Federal Law Enforcement Careers, Testing & Interviewing Guide

The information contained in this book has been obtained from the Office of Personnel Management and other reliable sources. Application procedures, qualifications, salaries, entrance examinations, interviewing questions, etc. are always subject to change. Therefore, you should contact the agencies you are interested in to obtain the most current information.

Published by
PoliceEmployment.com
P.O. Box 2090
Winterville, NC 28590-2090

ISBN: 0-9679998-3-9
Library of Congress Card Number: 2001086284

Federal Law Enforcement, Careers, Testing, & Interviewing Guide.

First Edition
Manufactured in the United States of America
1 2 3 4 5 6 7 8 9 10
Morris Publishing • 3212 East Highway 30 • Kearney, NE 68847
1-800-650-7888

To the men and women who keep our country safe.

Contents

General Information about Federal Law Enforcement Jobs

Office of Personnel Management
The Office of Personnel Management (OPM) maintains Federal Job Information/ Testing Centers in several major metropolitan areas across the country to provide local job information. They are listed under "U.S. Government" in the white pages of area phone directories. Visit OPM's web site at http://www.usajobs.opm.gov where you can search for current job openings. You can also obtain application forms from OPM by calling their USAJOBS line at (202) 606-2700, or by calling their Telephone Application Processing System (TAPS) at (912) 757-3192.

The OPM accepts applications for Federal employment, based on the number of jobs Government agencies estimate they will fill in various locations over a period of time. After you apply, the OPM examiners evaluate your application to see whether you are qualified for the same kinds of jobs. When government hiring officials have vacancies, they may ask the OPM for the names of people qualified for the jobs. The best qualified peoples' names are referred from the OPM for consideration by the agency.

Most Federal Law Enforcement jobs are in the competitive service, which means that people applying for them must be evaluated by OPM. OPM may authorize the hiring agency to examine applicants' qualifications. In that case you apply directly with the agency. Some agencies are exempt from OPM competitive service procedures. If you are interested in an exempt service job, you should not apply through OPM, but you should contact the agency directly.

Standard Form 171 - Application for Federal Employment
This is usually collected the day you take the written examination administered by OPM. Some agencies may require that you mail it directly to them. The SF-171 contains your education, work experience, special skill, references, military service, availability and general information. Some agencies may accept a resume or an Optional Form 612 in lieu of a 171.

Transfer Eligibility

If you are already a Federal employee, you may be eligible to transfer from one position to another position. Eligibility for transfer is based on prior career-conditional or career appointments in competitive positions. Generally, you do not have to take the written test and you apply directly to the hiring agency. You cannot transfer from an exempt position to a competitive position. The application procedures outlined in this booklet apply to those candidates who are not currently employed by the Federal government.

Overtime

In addition to an annual salary, most Agents and Officers can earn a considerable amount of money by working overtime hours. A lot of agencies pay overtime in the form of Availability Pay. Beginning October 1995, the Law Enforcement Availability Pay (LEAP) Bill took effect. LEAP gives 1811 Criminal Investigators 25% of their base salary in overtime regardless of how many hours they work in a pay period.

LEAP is good in that the overtime earned counts toward your retirement. LEAP can be bad in that it is limited to 25% of your base salary. Therefore, it is possible to work more hours than what you are actually being paid.

For other agencies, overtime is compensated at the rate of time and one half. This is good in that you get paid for every overtime hour worked. (There is a limit on how much you can earn in a pay period.) Time and one half compensation is bad in that generally any overtime money earned does not count toward your retirement. Some agencies allow their employees to earn compensatory time off for overtime worked.

Benefits

Federal employment provides many benefits, including vacation, sick leave, life and health insurance, and a liberal retirement plan. Benefits will vary slightly from agency to agency. In general, federal law enforcement benefits are as follows:

Annual Leave - In the private sector, this is referred to as "vacation time." Instead of getting a certain number of weeks per year, annual leave is accrued by a certain number of hours per pay period (every two weeks). The first three years of federal service you receive four hours per pay period. Three to fifteen years of federal service you receive six hours per pay period. Fifteen years and up you receive eight hours per pay period. You may carry over up to 240 hours of annual leave from one year to the next year.

Sick Leave - Accrued at the rate of four hours per pay period regardless of how many years of service you have. There is no limit to how many hours of sick leave you can accumulate.

Life Insurance - A basic life insurance policy is offered. However, you can probably do better to invest your money in a life insurance policy outside of the federal government. There are some benefits paid out if you are killed in the line of duty.

Health Insurance - The federal government pays for part of your health insurance premium. You pay the rest of the premium. You can choose from several plans and every year you have the opportunity to switch to a different plan to meet your health insurance needs.

Retirement Plan - All new employees are under the Federal Employees Retirement System (FERS). This is a three-part system involving social security, a thrift savings plan, and a federal retirement plan. Employees who have at least 20 years of federal law enforcement service are eligible for special retirement at age 50. Mandatory retirement is at age 57.

General Schedule Pay Chart

Most Federal Agencies pay their employees according to the General Schedule Pay Chart. Most positions start at a GS-5 or GS-7 (Step One) grade level. After successfully completing one year at a lower grade, you are then promoted to the next highest grade. The journeyman grade level is the highest grade you can receive on a noncompetitive basis. To be promoted beyond the journeyman grade level, you must compete in the Merit Promotion System. Normal grade progression is GS-5, GS-7, GS-9, GS-11, GS-12, GS-13, etc. If you do not receive a grade increase after a one year period, you will receive a within-grade step increase. For example, if you were a GS-11 Step 1 for one year and did not receive a promotion to a grade GS-12, you would receive a step increase making you a GS-11 Step 2. Before moving from Steps 1-3 you must remain at each of those steps for one year. For steps 4-6, before moving up you must remain at each of those steps for two years. For steps 7-9, before moving up you must remain at each of those steps for three years.

The General Schedule is based on locality. There are separate GS pay scales for various localities. Federal employees working in New York City will earn a slightly higher salary then those individuals working in Peoria, Illinois. The schedule included with this guide applies to the majority of the United States and is called the "Rest Of Us" (RUS). This is for those individuals who work in a city that is not considered a high cost of living area. If you will be working in a high populated area, contact the agency you are interested in or OPM to find the appropriate General Schedule.

The current General Schedule can be found on our web site at http://www.PoliceEmployment.com/generalschedule

Chapter I
Federal Law Enforcement Careers

United States Secret Service
Special Agent

Special Agents of the United States Secret Services are charged with two missions: protection and investigations. Special Agents are authorized by law to protect:

- the President, the Vice President, the President-elect,
- the Vice President-elect and their immediate families;
- former Presidents and their spouses;
- visiting heads of foreign states or governments;
- major Presidential and vice-presidential candidates.

The Secret Service was established in 1865 for the sole purpose of suppressing the counterfeiting of U.S. currency. Today this remains a primary responsibility of Special Agents. The Secret Service is responsible for the investigation of stolen or forged U.S. Government checks and bonds. Agents also investigate major cases involving: credit and debit card fraud, computer fraud, automated teller machine fraud, and electronic transfer fraud.

Qualifications
A bachelor's degree from an accredited college or university in any field of study, or three years of law enforcement experience preferably in criminal investigation meets the minimum educational requirements. Applicants will also be accepted if they possess a comparable combination of experience and education. You must pass an interview, a polygraph examination and a background investigation. All appointees must be 21 to 36 years old at the time of entrance on duty. Applicants must pass a medical examination provided by the Secret Service. Distant vision must be 20/60 in each eye uncorrected and 20/20 in each eye corrected.

Training
All agents receive nine weeks of criminal investigative training at the Federal Law Enforcement Training Center in Glynco, Georgia, and approximately eight weeks of specialized instruction at Secret Service training facilities in the Washington, D.C. area. Training includes courses in protective techniques, criminal law, the use of

firearms, defensive measures, surveillance techniques and undercover operations.

Salary
Special Agents begin at a GS-5, GS-7 or GS-9 grade level depending on your qualifications. The full performance level for a Special Agent is GS-13. Positions above the GS-13 level are based on merit promotions.

How To Apply
Candidates must pass the Treasury Enforcement Agent Examination. Candidates may apply at the nearest OPM office or at the nearest Secret Service field office.

For additional information contact the U.S. Secret Service Personnel Division, 905 H. Street, N.W., Washington, D.C. 20001-4518 or call their job hotline at 1 888 813-8777, or visit their internet site at http://www.treas.gov/usss

United States Secret Service Uniformed Division Police Officer

The United States Secret Service Uniformed Division has one mission - protection. Providing protection for the President and First Family while in residence at the White House remains the primary mission of the Secret Service Uniformed Division. Uniformed Division Officers also provide protection for the official residence of the Vice President, building in which Presidential offices are located, and foreign diplomatic missions in the Washington, D.C. area.

Uniformed Division Officers carry out their protective responsibilities through a network of vehicular patrols, foot patrols and fixed posts. They provide additional assistance to the overall Secret Service protective mission through canine, magnetometer and counter-sniper programs.

Qualifications
You must be a United States citizen and at least 21 to 36 years old by the time of appointment. You must possess a high school diploma or equivalent. Upon passing a written exam, qualified applicants will then receive a personal interview. Applicants must pass a comprehensive physical examination. Vision must be at least 20/60 in each eye, correctable to 20/20. Selected applicants must pass a background investigation and complete a polygraph.

Training
New appointees receive eight weeks of training at the Federal Law Enforcement Training Center in Glynco, Georgia and approximately seven weeks of instruction at Secret Service training facilities in the Washington, D.C. area. Training includes course work in police procedures, criminal law, laws of arrest, search and seizure, physical defense techniques, firearms and physical fitness.

Salary
The Uniformed Division has its own pay scale. Officers start at around $35,000 with annual raises over a three-year period. Opportunities for promotions exist on a competitive basis.

How To Apply
Testing and interviewing are conducted by Secret Service personnel. The examination is usually given on a quarterly basis in the Washington, D.C. area and periodically in other major U.S. cities. To apply, submit an SF-171 or an OF-612. You can also submit a resume and an OF-306 Declaration for Federal Employment.

To register your card or for further information contact the U.S. Secret Service, Attn: Uniformed Division Recruiter, 1310 L. St., Suite 400, N.W., Washington, D.C. 20223 or call their job hotline at 1 888 813-8777, or visit their internet site at http://www.treas.gov/usss

Bureau of Alcohol, Tobacco and Firearms Special Agent

ATF Special Agents investigate violations of Federal Explosive laws, including most bombings and many arson-for-profit schemes affecting interstate commerce. ATF Special Agents also investigate violations of Federal firearm's laws in an effort to prevent illicit trafficking, illegal possession and criminal use of firearms. Other ATF responsibilities are to investigate violations of the Federal Alcohol Administration Act, illicit liquor violations of Federal magnitude and interstate smugglers of non-tax-paid cigarettes. These investigations include surveillance, participating in raids, interviewing suspects and witnesses, making arrests, obtaining search warrants and searching for physical evidence.

Qualifications
Candidates must be a U. S. citizen and at least 21 but less than 37 years of age. They must be able to pass a background investigation, a comprehensive medical exam and drug screening exam. Distant vision without correction must be at least 20/100 in each eye, corrected to 20/20 in one eye and 20/30 in the other eye. Candidates must have a four-year college degree. Three years of law enforcement experience may be substituted for the educational requirements at the GS-5 level.

Training
Appointees undergo approximately nine weeks of criminal investigative training in general law enforcement and investigative techniques at the Federal Law Enforcement Training Center in Glynco, Georgia. Subjects of study include: surveillance techniques, rules of evidence, undercover assignments, arrest techniques and the use of firearms.

Agents later attend 13 weeks of New Agent Training at the FLETC where they receive highly specialized training in their duties as ATF agents. Subjects studied relate to the laws enforced by ATF, firearms and explosive nomenclature, bomb scene search and arson training.

Salary
Initial appointments are generally made at the GS-5 or GS-7 level. Career progression to GS-9, GS-11, GS-12 and journeyman GS-13 generally follows at one-year intervals. Thereafter, promotions to higher grades are on a competitive basis.

How To Apply
Special Agent candidates must pass the Treasury Enforcement Agent Examination given by the Office of Personnel Management.

For further information contact the Bureau of Alcohol, Tobacco and Firearms, Personnel Division, Room 4100, 650 Massachusetts Ave., N.W., Washington, D.C. 20226 or call their personnel number at (202) 927-5690 / 8610 or visit their internet site at http://www.atf.treas.gov

Federal Bureau of Investigation Special Agent

The Federal Bureau of Investigation serves as the investigative arm of the United States Department of Justice with jurisdiction in more than 260 types of cases. The work of a Special Agent includes investigation into organized crime, white-collar crime, public corruption, bribery, civil rights violations, bank robbery, kidnaping, terrorism and other violations of Federal statutes.

Qualifications
You must be a U.S. citizen at least 23 but less than 37 years of age, have uncorrected vision not less than 20/200 and corrected 20/20 in one eye and at least 20/40 in the other eye, pass a physical examination, drug test, polygraph examination, score high on a formal interview and pass a background investigation.

There are four entrance programs under which Special Agents qualify:

1. LAW - possess a JD degree from a resident law school.

2. ACCOUNTING - four year college or university degree in accounting.
3. LANGUAGE - four year college degree plus fluency in foreign language for which the Bureau has a current need.
4. DIVERSIFIED - four year college degree plus three years full-time work experience.

Training
Newly appointed Special Agents report to the FBI Academy at Quantico, Virginia where they undergo approximately 15 weeks of training. Training classes generally consist of academic and investigative instruction, defensive tactics, physical fitness and firearms training.

Salary
Successful applicants begin employment at the GS-10 level. Careers progress to a GS-13 level generally in three years.

How To Apply
Being an exempt agency not governed by the Office of Personnel Management appointment regulations, the FBI utilizes a centralized hiring system. Applications can be obtained from and should be submitted to the nearest FBI field office. Candidates will undergo an initial written examination and an interview.

For further information contact the nearest FBI field office in your area. The location of their field offices can be obtained from your local telephone directory, or call their employment hotline at (202) 324-3674, or visit their internet site at http://www.fbi.gov

United States Marshals Service
Deputy United States Marshal

The United States Marshals Service is the nation's oldest federal law enforcement agency. The backbone of the U.S. Marshals Service is the Deputy U.S. Marshal. Storied throughout history for legendary heroics in the face of lawlessness, Deputy U.S. Marshals pursue and arrest fugitives who have escaped from Federal custody, who have violated parole or probation conditions, or who have failed to appear before courts as ordered. They ensure a secure protection for Federal judges. They also transport Federal prisoners by land and air, serve processes, and run the Witness Security Program. Other duties require the Deputy U.S. Marshal to seize and manage assets acquired from criminal activities and quell civil disturbances.

Qualifications

You must be a U.S. citizen and not have reached your 37th birthday by the time of appointment. You must have a bachelor's degree or three years of responsible experience or an equivalent combination of education and experience. One academic year of full-time undergraduate study is equivalent to nine months of responsible experience. You must pass an oral interview, a physical examination and a Physical Efficiency Battery test. Vision must be at least 20/200 in each eye, correctable to 20/20. Applicants are subject to a personal background investigation to determine suitability for employment.

Training

Trainees are required to complete a 15-week basic training program consisting of a nine-week Criminal Investigator's course followed by six weeks of courses related to the specific duties of a Deputy U.S. Marshal at the Federal Law Enforcement Training Center in Glynco, Georgia. Advance training is available throughout a Deputy U.S. Marshal's career.

Salary

Based on educational and experience background, most initial appointments are at a grade GS-5 or GS-7. Deputies are eligible for promotions to GS-9 and GS-11 after successfully completing one year at the lower grade. After three years at a GS-11 level, deputies are promoted to a GS-12.

How To Apply

You must pass a written USMS examination administered by the Office of Personnel Management. Contact OPM or the nearest Marshals Service office for the next testing dates.

For further information contact the U.S. Marshals Service, Personnel Management Division, Law Enforcement Recruiting Branch, 600 Army Navy Drive, Arlington, VA 22202-4210 or call their testing information number (202) 307-9437, or visit their internet site at http://www.usdoj.gov/marshals

Drug Enforcement Administration Special Agent

The Drug Enforcement Administration is the primary federal law enforcement agency charged with the responsibility of combating drug abuse. The DEA enforces laws and statutes relating to narcotic drugs, marijuana, depressants, stimulants and hallucinogenic drugs. Its objectives are to reach all levels of source of supply and to interdict illegal drugs before they reach the user. Special Agents conduct criminal investigations and prepare for the prosecution of major violators of the drugs laws of the United States. Senior Special Agents may volunteer for overseas assignments.

Qualifications

You must be at least 21 and less than 37 years of age at the time of appointment. You must pass an oral interview, a background investigation, a polygraph exam and psychological exam. Uncorrected vision of at least 20/200 in both eyes, corrected to 20/20 in one eye and 20/40 in the other. RK surgery is not permitted. You must possess a college degree in any field and one year of experience conducting criminal investigations or comparable experience, or a college degree in any field or substantive professional / administrative or law enforcement experience.

Training

Selected applicants attend approximately 16 weeks of basic training at the FBI Academy in Quantico, Virginia. Some of the courses of study are: narcotic laws, arrest techniques, surveillance techniques, search and seizure laws, firearms use, practical exercises and self defense.

Salary
Entry level salary is at the GS-7 or GS-9 level, depending on the applicant's qualifications. Careers generally progress to the GS-12 level in three years. Agents are then eligible for promotions to the GS-13 level and above.

How To Apply
There is no written test for the Special Agent position. DEA has direct hire authority so you apply directly to the DEA. Submit a Personal Qualifications Statement (SF-171), a Background Survey Questionnaire (OPM Form 1386) and a complete college transcript to the DEA office nearest you.

For further information contact the Drug Enforcement Administration, Office of Personnel, 1405 I Street N.W., Washington, D.C. 20537, call their job hotline (800) DEA-4288 or visit their internet site at http://www.usdoj.gov/dea

United States Department of State Special Agent

Special Agents for the Department of State perform several duties including protection and investigation. Special Agents are responsible for protecting foreign dignitaries as well as high ranking Department of State officials. Special Agents have primary jurisdiction in conducting criminal investigations concerning passport fraud and visa fraud. Special Agents also conduct background investigations on Department of State employees.

Every five years Special Agents are assigned to an overseas embassy or consulate for approximately two years as a Security Officer responsible for the security of the embassy and/or consulate.

Qualifications

You must possess a bachelor's degree plus one year of work experience or educational equivalent. You must be 21 to 36 years old, pass a background investigation, a physical examination and a drug screening exam. Your distant vision must be correctable to 20/20.

Training

Selected applicants attend approximately nine weeks of Criminal Investigative training at the Federal Law Enforcement Training Center in Glynco, Georgia. Upon graduation from the FLETC, candidates attend nine to 12 weeks of training specific to their duties in the Washington, D.C. area. Additional training is required for those Agents assigned to overseas duty stations.

Salary

Special Agents are paid according to the Foreign Service pay scale. Special Agents generally begin at an FP-6 level which is between $30,000 - $42,000 per year. Special Agents receive two grade increases over the next two and one half years. Promotions thereafter are on a competitive basis.

How To Apply

You apply directly to the Department of State. You must send them a completed Application for Federal Employment, DS-1950, a 2 - 3 page typed and double-spaced biography of yourself and a copy of your college transcripts. When the Department of State is hiring, applicants will be scheduled for a written essay test and an oral interview. If you pass the essay and interview, you will be placed on a register of eligible applicants for eighteen months.

For further information write to the Recruitment Division, U.S. Department of State, P.O. Box 9317, Arlington, VA 22219 or call their Foreign Service Career Line at (703) 875-7490 or visit their internet site at http://www.heroes.net or http://www.state.gov/www/careers/index.html

Fish and Wildlife Service Special Agent

The U. S. Fish and Wildlife Service is the principal agency through which the Federal Government carries out its responsibilities for managing the Nation's wild birds, mammals and fish. Special Agents investigate violations of Federal Law involving the protection and conservation of wild life, including birds, mammals, reptiles, mollusks, fish and crustacea. Investigations involve surveillance, participation in raids, interviewing witnesses, interrogating suspects, searching for physical evidence, seizures of contraband and making arrests.

Qualifications

Three years of general experience or a four-year degree from an accredited college or university in any major field of study qualifies an applicant for a Special Agent position. Applicants must be 21, but less than 37 years of age and pass a full field investigation which may be conducted either before or after appointment. Pre-employment medical exams are at the expense of the candidate. Distant vision must test at least 20/200 in each eye without correction and at least 20/20 in one eye and 20/30 in the other eye with correction.

Training

Upon initial appointment, Special Agents attend approximately 14 weeks of formal training in law enforcement techniques at the Federal Law Enforcement Training Center in Glynco, Georgia. Training includes: rules of evidence, report preparation, investigative techniques, applicable laws and court decisions. Following formal classroom training, Agents are assigned to one of seven designated law enforcement districts for "on the job" training throughout the United States. Generally, twelve to eighteen months after initial employment, a Special Agent is transferred to one of a number of law enforcement districts located throughout the country.

Salary

Initial appointments are at a grade GS-5, GS-7 or GS-9 depending on your experience and education qualifications. Opportunities exist for positions at the GS-11 level and above.

How To Apply

Candidates are recruited by the OPM. OPM may announce its recruitment through one of its standard Examination Announcements or through a special Recruitment Bulletin. A candidate may call any FWS personnel office to find out whether FWS plans to ask OPM for a list of qualified candidates.

For further information contact the United States Fish and Wildlife Service, 4401 N. Fairfax Drive, Room 500, Arlington, VA 22203 or call (703) 358-1949 or visit their internet site at http://www.fws.gov

United States Naval Criminal Investigative Service
Special Agent

Naval Criminal Investigative Service Special Agents are the successors of the operatives and agents who served as part of the Office of Naval Intelligence (ONI) in World War I. Special Agents investigate crimes committed by or against Department of Navy personnel. These crimes include homicide, rape, arson, robbery and narcotic trafficking. Special Agents may service aboard an aircraft carrier with the responsibility of investigating crimes on the carrier and on all other ships of the accompanying battle group. Special Agents also work on counterintelligence and performing protective assignments. During a 20-year career Special Agents can expect to do at least two tours of duty overseas.

Qualifications

You must be a U.S. citizen 21 to 37 years old with a bachelor's degree from an accredited college or university. You must pass a physical examination and have uncorrected vision no greater than

20/200, correctable to 20/20 in one eye and 20/30 in the other. Applicants must also pass an extensive background investigation.

Training
Prospective agents must complete approximately 16 weeks of basic training at the Federal Law Enforcement Training Center in Glynco, Georgia. Subjects of study include law enforcement, practical exercises, physical specialties and firearms. Agents also receive NCIS Agent training.

Salary
Initial appointments are at a GS-7 grade level. Noncompetitive annual grade increases are given over a three-year period until Agents reach the GS-13 grade level.

How To Apply
Submit a completed SF-171 to the nearest Naval Investigative Office in your area. You can write to their main office in Washington, D.C. to obtain the address of the NIS Regional office nearest you or visit their web site.

For further information contact the Naval Criminal Investigative Service, Career Services Department, Building 200, Washington Navy Yard Building, Washington, D.C. 20374 or call 1 800 616-8891, or visit their internet site at http://www.ncis.navy.mil

United States Postal Service
Postal Inspector

The protection of the U.S. Mail and the mail system is the responsibility of the Postal Inspection Service. Postal Inspectors are the fact finding and investigative agents of the U.S. Postal Service. Postal Inspectors investigate violations of all postal laws such as mail fraud, the illegal transmission of controlled substances through the U.S. Mail, the mailing of child pornography, thefts of mail, bombs sent through the mail, the mailing of matter containing poison, and assault on postal employees. Inspectors apprehend violators of such laws.

Qualifications

Applicants must be U.S. citizens with a minimum age of 21 and a maximum age of 36. You must have a baccalaureate degree, any major from an accredited college or university. You must also meet one of the following special requirements:

-Postal Service employees with two years of supervisory, inspection or specialized experience;

-two years of conducting internal audits;

-two years of law enforcement experience;

-two years of military service;

-possess foreign language expertise.

You must pass a medical examination, background investigation, drug screening, polygraph exam and an oral interview. Uncorrected vision must be at least 20/100 in each eye, correctable to 20/30 in one eye and 20/40 in the other.

Training

All trainees undergo a sixteen-week basic training course involving use of firearms, defensive tactics, legal matters, search and seizure, arrest techniques, court procedure, postal operations and audit functions. Classes are conducted at the Inspection Service training center in Potomac, Maryland.

Salary

Postal employee salaries correspond to the Executive Administrative Schedule (EAS). Inspectors generally start at an EAS-17 which is around $46,000. Promotion to EAS-19, EAS-21 and EAS-23 generally follow at one year intervals.

How To Apply

Write to the Postal Service Personnel Division. They will send you a questionnaire and an Application for Employment. Qualified applicants will be notified when and where an examination will be administered.

For further information call (301) 983-7400 or write to the U.S. Postal Inspection Service, Career Development Division, 9600

Newbridge Drive, Potomac, MD 20858-4328. Visit their internet site at http:www.usps.gov/websites/depart/inspect

Internal Revenue Service Special Agent

The Internal Revenue Service collects more than 90% of the Federal tax revenue, thereby ensuring the existence of all types of vital Federal programs. Special Agents investigate charges of criminal and civil violations on Internal Revenue laws, generally involving tax fraud. Special Agents may conduct surveillance, serve as a witness in criminal and civil trials and participate in making arrests.

Qualifications

You must have three years of accounting or related business experience or a bachelor's degree if your studies included at least 24 semester hours of accounting, business law or finance courses, of which at least 15 semester hours are in accounting. You must not have reached your 37th birthday in order to be considered for this job. You must pass a background investigation and a physical examination. Uncorrected distant vision must test at least 20/200, correctable to at least 20/20 in one eye and 20/30 in the other eye.

Training

Agents receive nine weeks of general criminal investigative training at the Federal Law Enforcement Training Center in Glynco, GA. After completing this program, agents then receive an additional 16 weeks of specialized IRS training.

Salary

Initial appointments are generally made at a GS-5 or GS-7 grade level depending on your qualifications. You will generally be promoted until you reach the full working level of GS-12. Opportunities to advance to a higher level exist on a competitive basis.

How To Apply
You must take the Treasury Enforcement Agent Examination. You should contact the IRS Recruitment Coordinator nearest you for test scheduling and to obtain forms needed to complete your application.

For further information contact your local IRS office or write the IRS Centralized Examination Unit, 290 Broadway, 13th Floor, New York, NY 10008 or call them at (212) 436-1403 or visit their internet site at http://www.ustreas.gov/irs/ci/index.htm

United States Customs Service Special Agent

The U.S. Customs Service was created by the first Congress of the United States in 1789. The U.S. Custom Service protects the American public, labor and business by enforcing trademark, copyright and patent privileges. Special Agents investigate violations encompassing a wide variety of laws concerning the illegal shipment of arms and high technology to foreign entities, the illicit transportation of currency in support of criminal enterprise, and schemes to defraud the U.S. Government of revenue. Special Agents have the authority to search and make arrests and to seize and confiscate smuggled articles or contraband.

Qualifications
You must be a U.S. citizen under the age of 37. You must pass a physical examination, a background investigation and a drug test. You must have one year of general experience and two years of specialized experience or four years of study in an accredited college leading to a bachelor's degree in any field of study.

Training
Candidates must successfully complete approximately 17 weeks of enforcement training at the Federal Law Enforcement Training Center in Glynco, Georgia. This consists of written and physical

tests, as well as graded practical exercises including one on firearms proficiency.

Salary
Appointments are made at the GS-5 and GS-7 entry depending on your qualifications. Opportunities exist for advancement to higher grade levels on a competitive basis. This position has a journeyman level of GS-12.

How To Apply
You must establish an eligible rating on the OPM register of eligibles for the position and grade level for which you are qualified. You must pass the Treasury Enforcement Agent (TEA) Examination administered by OPM.

For further information contact the U.S. Customs Service, Office of Human Resources, 1300 Pennsylvania Ave., N.W., Washington, D.C. 20229 or call their job hotline at 1 800 944-7725, or visit their internet site at http://www.customs.gov

United States Customs Service
Import Specialist

Import Specialists decide whether arriving commercial cargo and shipments are admissible into the country. Once admissibility is established, they decide how that merchandise should be classified and appraised under tariff laws. Import Specialists help protect business and labor by enforcing a wide variety of statutes, regulations and executive orders. These range from fair trade laws, copyright and trademark laws, laws on the marking of the country of origin and many more. Specialists also work with special enforcement teams that investigate fraud, negligence, and complicated efforts to get around tariff and trade laws.

Qualifications
You must be a U.S. citizen under the age of 37. You must pass a physical examination and a background investigation. You must

have at least three years of progressively responsible work experience. One year of college equals nine months of work experience. A bachelor's degree is fully qualifying for a GS-5 level.

Training
Candidates must successfully complete approximately seven weeks of technical training at the Federal Law Enforcement Training Center in Glynco, Georgia. This consists of written as well as graded practical exercises.

Salary
Entrance level appointments are made generally at the GS-5 level and occasionally at the GS-7 level, depending on your qualifications. The position offers advancement potential to the journeyman level at GS-11 with positions available at grade GS-12 and above on a competitive basis.

How To Apply
You must establish an eligible rating on the OPM ACWA Examination for Law Enforcement and Investigative positions. Submit OPM Form 5000-B, Admission Notice and Record Card, to the OPM office nearest you. The admission notice will be returned to you telling you when and where to report for the test.

If you are a college graduate who obtained a grade point average of 3.4 or higher on a 4.0 scale for all undergraduate courses completed toward a baccalaureate degree, or if you stand in the upper 10% of a baccalaureate grading class, you are eligible for the Outstanding Scholar Program. You need not take the written ACWA exam.

For further information contact the U.S. Customs Service, Office of Human Resources, 1300 Pennsylvania Ave, N.W., Washington, D.C. 20229 or their job hotline at 1 800 944-7725, or visit their internet site at http://www.customs.gov

United States Customs Service
Customs Inspector

Customs Inspectors process persons, baggage, cargo and mail, as well as administer certain navigation laws. To insure compliance with tariff laws and to prevent smuggling, fraud and cargo theft, uniformed Customs Inspectors review the individual baggage declarations of international travelers and oversee the unloading of all types of commercial shipments. As part of the customs law enforcement team, Inspectors search persons, cargo, ships, aircraft, cars and other vehicles, seize contraband and apprehend violators.

Qualifications
You must be a U.S. citizen and pass a physical examination, a background investigation and a drug test. You must have three years of responsible experience equivalent to a GS-4. A bachelor's degree meets all of the experience requirements.

Training
Candidates must successfully complete approximately 11 weeks of enforcement training at the Federal Law Enforcement Training Center in Glynco, Georgia. This consists of written and physical tests as well as graded practical exercises, including one on firearms proficiency.

Salary
Entrance level appointments are generally made at the grade GS-5 level and occasionally at the GS-7 level, depending on your qualifications. Opportunities exist for advancement to the journeyman level at grade GS-9, with opportunities also existing to apply for senior level positions at grade GS-11 and above.

How To Apply
You must establish an eligible rating on the OPM Administrative Careers with America (ACWA) Examination for Law Enforcement and Investigative Positions. This includes an oral exam administered by the Customs Service.

If you are a college graduate who obtained a grade point average of 3.4 or higher on a 4.0 scale for all undergraduate courses completed toward a baccalaureate degree, or if you stand in the upper 10% of a baccalaureate graduating class, you are eligible for the Outstanding Scholar Program. You need not take the written ACWA exam.

For further information contact the U.S. Customs Service, Office of Human Resources, 1300 Pennsylvania Ave., N.W., Washington, D.C. 20229 or call their job hotline at 1 800 944-7725, or visit their internet site at http://www.customs.gov

United States Customs Service Canine Enforcement Officer

Canine Enforcement Officers (CEO's) train and use dogs to enforce Custom laws and regulations concerning the smuggling of narcotics and dangerous drugs. CEO's work in cooperation with Special Agents, Customs Inspectors and Customs Investigators to interdict all types of controlled substances and to apprehend, search and arrest suspected smugglers. CEO's are assigned to various air, sea and land border ports of entry throughout the United States.

Qualifications

You must be a U.S. citizen and pass a physical examination, a background investigation and a drug test. You must have at least three years of responsible experience. A bachelor's degree meets all the experience requirements.

Training

Candidates must successfully complete approximately 15 weeks of enforcement and dog handler training conducted at the U.S. Customs Service Canine Enforcement Training Center located in Front Royal, VA. This consists of written and physical tests, as well as graded practical exercises, including one on firearms proficiency.

Salary
Initial appointments are generally made at the GS-5 level, with an opportunity to advance to the GS-9 level. Beyond grade GS-9, possibilities for advancement to higher grade levels exist on a competitive basis.

How To Apply
The OPM issues recruitment bulletins when the Customs Service is hiring for the position of Canine Enforcement Officer. No written test is required. Candidates are rated on their education, experience and background as reflected on their application forms.

For further information contact the U.S. Customs Service, Office of Human Resources, 1300 Pennsylvania Ave., N.W., Washington, D.C. 20229 or call their job hotline at 1 800 944-7725, or visit their internet site at http://www.customs.gov

United States Customs Service
Customs Pilot

Customs Pilots perform flight duties in support of a program primarily involving air surveillance of illegal traffic crossing U.S. borders by air, land or sea. Customs' fleet of specially fitted interdiction aircraft pursues would-be smugglers to remote landing spots in difficult terrain. Pilots apprehend, arrest and search violators of Customs and related laws. Pilots can be employed in a variety of Air Support Branches throughout the country.

Qualifications
You must be a U.S. citizen under the age of 37. You must have a current FAA Class II physical examination. You must also pass a background investigation and a drug test. You must have a current FAA commercial pilot's license with 1500 flight time hours.

Training
Candidates must successfully complete approximately 16 weeks of enforcement training at the Federal Law Enforcement Training

Center in Glynco, Georgia. This consists of written and physical tests, as well as graded practical exercises, including one on firearms proficiency.

Salary

Initial appointments to Pilot positions are made at the GS-11 level, with noncompetitive promotion to the GS-12 level. Opportunities also exist for GS-13 level positions.

How To Apply

No test is required; you will be rated on the basis of your experience as it is reflected on your application (SF-171) and Record of Aeronautical Experience (OPM-1170-21). These forms should be submitted directly to the U.S. Customs Service for eligibility determination.

For further information contact the U.S. Customs Service, Office of Human Resources, 1300 Pennsylvania Avenue, Room 2.5B, N.W., Washington, D.C. 20044 or call their job hotline at 1 800 944-7725, or visit their internet site at http://www.customs.gov

Bureau of Land Management Criminal Investigator

The Bureau of Land Management is a bureau of the U.S. Department of the Interior. BLM is responsible for managing federally owned public lands consisting of forests and ranges. BLM Criminal Investigators are responsible for investigating various crimes committed on BLM properties. Natural resource crimes such as the removal of illegal timber and archeological crimes such as the theft of archeological artifacts are some of the offenses under BLM jurisdiction. BLM criminal investigators also operate a drug eradication program.

Qualifications

You must have a four-year degree from an accredited college or university, or an appropriate amount of experience. You must pass a physical examination and a background investigation. You must be between the ages of 21 and 37 at the time of appointment.

Training
Selected applicants attend a nine-week Criminal Investigators training course conducted at the Federal Law Enforcement Training Center in Glynco, Georgia. Those applicants who have criminal investigator experience may attend a shortened five week training course.

Salary
Initial appointments are generally made at the GS-5 or GS-7 grade level depending on your qualifications. Annual grade increases are received up to the GS-12 journeyman level. Opportunities exist for competitive promotions beyond the GS-12 grade level.

How To Apply
The Bureau of Land Management hires Criminal Investigators based on experience and training. Many of these positions are filled through federal transfers. There is no written test. You must submit a Standard Form 171 to apply.

For further information contact the U.S. Department of the Interior, Bureau of Land Management, Personnel Services, 18th & C Streets N.W., Washington, D.C. 20240, or call their Human Resources Office at (703) 440-1500, their Colorado Job Hotline number (303) 236-6706, or visit their internet site at http://www.blm.gov

National Park Service
Park Ranger (Law Enforcement)

The National Park Service is a Bureau of the U.S. Department of the Interior. Since its creation in 1916, it has been preserving, protecting and managing the natural, cultural, historical and recreational areas of the National Park System. Park Rangers supervise, manage and perform work in the conservation and use of resources in national parks. Park Rangers carry out various tasks associated with forest or structural fire control; protection of property; gathering and dissemination of natural, historical, or scientific information; enforcement of laws and regulations; investigation of violations, complaints and accidents; apprehension of violators; and performance of searches and rescues.

Qualifications and Salary

GS-2 - Graduation from a full 4-year or senior high school or possession of a GED.

GS-3 - One year of general experience or completion of one year of college.

GS-4 - One year of specialized experience or completion of two years of college.

GS-5 - Two years of specialized experience or a bachelor's degree from an accredited college.

You must be at least 21 years of age and be in excellent physical condition. You should have vision correctable to 20/30 in each eye.

Training

Park Rangers receive training for duties unique to the Park Service at the Horace M. Albright Training Center at Grand Canyon National Park, AZ or at the Stephen T. Mather Training Center at Harpers Ferry, WV. In addition, the Park Service makes use of the Federal Law Enforcement Training Center in Glynco, Georgia. Training generally lasts for 17 weeks.

How To Apply

Park Ranger positions are filled in accordance with the Office of Personnel Management regulations. You may have to take the appropriate examination administered by OPM, or the Regional NPS Office may request authorization from OPM to hire from among those persons who apply directly to the NPS.

For further information contact the National Park Service, 1849 C. St., N.W., Washington, D.C. 20240 or call (202) 208-6843, or visit their internet site at http://www.nps.gov/personnel

National Park Service
United States Park Police Officer

U.S. Park Police Officers are employed by the National Capitol Region, National Park Service, Department of Interior. U.S. Park Police Officers preserve the peace; prevent, detect and investigate crimes; arrest violators and often provide crowd control at large public gatherings. The U.S. Park Police force includes horse mounted, motorcycle, vehicular, helicopter and canine units. U.S. Park Police Officers are usually assigned to the Washington, D.C., New York City or San Francisco areas.

Qualifications

You must have completed two years of college studies or have two years of responsible experience. You must be between the ages of 21 and 35, pass a background investigation, a physical battery test, a physical examination and an oral interview. Your uncorrected distant vision must be 20/100 or better, correctable to 20/20.

Training

U.S. Park Police Officers attend approximately 18 weeks of training at the Federal Law Enforcement Training Center in Glynco, Georgia. Upon graduation from FLETC, the recruit officer will undergo additional training under the guidance of an experienced field training officer.

Salary

The U.S. Park Police has its own pay scale. In the Washington, D.C. area, officers begin at around $34,000 per year with annual increases. Opportunities exist for promotions to higher grade levels.

How To Apply

You must take the appropriate civil service test given by the Office of Personnel Management. Military personnel may apply to the Office of Personnel Management to take the examination within 120 days prior to or within 120 days after honorable discharge.

For further information write to the U.S. Park Police, Personnel Office, 1100 Ohio Drive S.W., Washington, D.C. 20242 or call their personnel office at (202) 619-7056, or visit their internet site at http://www.doi.gov/usparkpolice

United States Immigration and Naturalization Service Special Agent

The Immigration and Naturalization Service enforces our Nation's Immigration and Nationality laws. Special Agents plan and conduct investigations concerning the criminal and statutory provisions of the Immigration and Nationality laws. Special Agents carry firearms, make arrests, prepare investigative reports and present cases to the U.S. Attorney for prosecution. Special Agents cooperate and maintain a liaison with federal and local agencies. Special Agents are located throughout the United States with larger offices in metropolitan areas.

Qualifications
You must be a U.S. citizen and at least 21 but less than 37 years of age at the time of appointment. You must pass a background investigation and be in excellent physical condition. You must have a bachelor's degree or three years of responsible experience. An equivalent combination of education and experience will also meet the requirements.

Training
Special Agents attend approximately 21 weeks of training at the Federal Law Enforcement Training Center in Glynco, Georgia. Agents study Immigration and Naturalization Laws, criminal law, defensive measures, surveillance techniques, pursuit driving, arrest techniques and the use of firearms.

Salary
Initial appointments are at grade GS-5 or GS-7 depending on the applicant's qualifications. Career progression to grades GS-9, GS-

11 and journeyman GS-12 generally follow at one year intervals. Thereafter, promotions to higher grades are made on a competitive basis.

How To Apply
You must establish an eligible rating with the Office of Personnel Management. This is done through either a written test or by filling out a questionnaire that reflects your previous experience.

For further information contact the Immigration and Naturalization Service, Personnel Division, 800 K Street, 5th Floor, Washington, D.C. 20536 or call (202) 514-2530, or visit their internet site at http://www.ins.usdoj.gov

United States Immigration and Naturalization Service Border Patrol Agent

The Border Patrol of the Immigration and Naturalization Service is a highly trained officer corp. As a mobile uniformed law enforcement organization, its primary mission is detecting and preventing the smuggling and illegal entry of persons into the United States. Border Patrol Agents are responsible for the apprehension of illegal aliens and smugglers of aliens at or near the land borders by maintaining surveillance from covert positions, following up leads, responding to electronic sensor alarms and aircraft sightings, and interpreting and following tracks, marks, and other physical evidence.

Qualifications
You must have a substantial amount of experience. You may substitute a full four-year course of college undergraduate study for experience. You must be younger than 37 at the time of appointment. You must be in excellent physical condition. Binocular vision is required and you must test 20/40 without corrective lenses. Uncorrected vision should be at least 20/70 in each eye. Vision in each eye must be corrected to 20/20. You must

pass an oral interview and a background investigation. The ability to read and speak Spanish at a level rated from good to excellent is required upon completion of the one year probationary period.

Training

Trainees undergo approximately 20 weeks of study at the Border Patrol Academy located at the Federal Law Enforcement Training Center in Glynco, Georgia. Some of the subjects trainees receive instruction in are: Immigration and Nationality Law, Report Writing, Methods of Tracking, Physical Training, Pursuit Driving, First Aid, Arrest Techniques, Firearms and Criminal Law. Trainees must also learn the Spanish language.

Salary

Entry level is grade GS-5 or GS-7 depending on your qualifications. Progression to grade GS-11 generally follows after one year at a GS-9. Opportunities for promotions exist on a competitive basis.

How To Apply

You have to take the appropriate civil service examination given by the Office of Personnel Management. For the latest information on testing, check with OPM or the Border Patrol. You can apply by telephone when they are hiring by calling 912 757-3001 extension 9916/9970. You can also apply online at their internet site.

For further information write to the Immigration and Naturalization Service, Border Patrol Examining Unit, 425 I Street N.W., 2nd Floor, Washington, D.C. 20536-0001, or call their personnel office at (202) 616-1964, or visit their internet site at http://www.ins.usdoj.gov

United States Immigration and Naturalization Service Immigration Agent

Immigration Agents (Enforcement) enforce laws and regulations under the Immigration and Nationality Act. This includes performing a variety of law enforcement and administrative tasks involving employer sanctions, criminal aliens, and the apprehension of absconders from deportation proceedings. Some of these positions are located in district offices and others at correction facilities.

Qualifications

You must be a U.S. citizen and at least 21 but less than 37 years of age at the time of appointment. You must pass a background investigation, an interview and be in excellent physical condition. You must have a bachelor's degree or three years of responsible experience. An equivalent combination of education and experience will also meet the requirements.

Training

Immigration Agents attend 17 weeks of training at the Federal Law Enforcement Training Center in Glynco, Georgia. Agents study Immigration and Naturalization Laws, constitutional law, criminal law, fugitive operations, behavioral science, defensive measures, arrest techniques, physical conditioning, use of firearms and the Spanish language.

Salary

Initial appointments are at grade GS-5 or GS-7 depending on the applicant's qualifications. Career progression is to the GS-9 level. Promotions to higher grades are made on a competitive basis.

How To Apply

You must establish an eligible rating with the Office of Personnel Management. This is done through either a written test or by filling out a questionnaire that reflects your previous experience.

For further information contact the Immigration and Naturalization Service, Personnel Division, 800 K Street, 5th Floor, Washington, D.C. 20536 or call (202) 514-2530, or visit their internet site at http://www.ins.usdoj.gov

United States Immigration and Naturalization Service Immigration Inspector

As millions of people enter the United States each year, the Immigrations Inspector is usually the first U.S. official that these people meet upon their arrival. Inspectors are stationed anywhere that people enter the United States from other countries - primarily land ports, seaports and airports. Inspectors are responsible for preventing ineligible persons from entering the United States. Inspectors must be guided in their work by a knowledge of controlling laws, regulations and policies, and court and administrative decisions.

Qualifications
You must be a U.S. citizen with a bachelor's degree or three years of responsible experience. You must possess emotional and mental stability and pass a physical examination and a background investigation. You must be at least 21 years old and under the age of 37.

Training
Selected applicants undergo approximately 17 weeks of intensive training at the Federal Law Enforcement Training Center in Glynco, Georgia. Training includes courses in the Spanish language, nationality laws, physical education and firearms proficiency.

Salary
Initial appointments are at grade GS-5. Career progression to grade GS-7, GS-9 and GS-11 requires a minimum of one year at each

grade level. Promotions to higher grades are made through competitive procedures of the Federal Merit Promotion System.

How To Apply

Contact the nearest INS office or the Office of Personnel Management for information on their current test and examination procedures.

For further information contact the INS regional office nearest you:

Eastern Region INS, 70 Kimball Avenue, South Burlington, VT 05403

Southern Region INS, 7701 North Stemmons Freeway, 1 Federal Drive, Dallas TX 76247

Northern Region INS, Federal Building, Fort Snelling, MN 55111

Western Region INS, 24000 Avila Rd., PO Box 30070, Laguna Niguel, CA 92607-0070

You can also call their personnel office at (202) 514-2530 or visit their internet site at http://www.ins.usdoj.gov

United States Immigration and Naturalization Service Deportation Officer

The Immigration and naturalization Services enforces our nation's laws regulating immigration and nationality matters. Under these laws it may become necessary to detain and/or deport certain individuals. The mission of the Deportation Officers is to provide for the control and removal of persons who have been ordered deported or otherwise required to depart from the United States. Officers must closely monitor deportation proceedings from initiation to conclusion. Close liaison with foreign consulates and embassies is required to facilitate the timely issuance of passports and travel documents required for deportation. Officers may be required to respond to congressional inquiries.

Qualifications
You must be a U.S. citizen and at least 21 but less than 37 years of age at the time of appointment. You must pass a background investigation, an interview and be in excellent physical condition. You must have a bachelor's degree or three years of responsible experience. An equivalent combination of education and experience will also meet the requirements.

Training
Deportation Officers attend 17 weeks of training at the Federal Law Enforcement Training Center in Glynco, Georgia. Agents study Immigration laws, alien removal process, fraudulent document detection, arrest techniques, escort and transportation, physical conditioning, use of firearms and the Spanish language.

Salary
Initial appointments are at grade GS-5 or GS-7 depending on the applicant's qualifications. Career progression is to the GS-11 level. Promotions to higher grades are available on a competitive basis.

How To Apply
You must establish an eligible rating with the Office of Personnel Management. This is done through either a written test or by filling out a questionnaire that reflects your previous experience.

For further information contact the Immigration and Naturalization Service, Personnel Division, 800 K Street, 5th Floor, Washington, D.C. 20536 or call (202) 514-2530, or visit their internet site at http://www.ins.usdoj.gov

United States Immigration and Naturalization Service Detention Enforcement Officer

Detention Enforcement Officers (DEO) perform a variety of tasks in Service Processing Facilities, Districts and/or Sectors. DEOs locate, apprehend, arrest, transport, safeguard, oversee/supervise and process aliens being detained and/or deported for violations of immigration laws. Aliens being detained and escorted represent a wide variety of individuals from countries all around the world who are subject to exclusion and deportation proceedings.

Qualifications

You must be a U.S. citizen and at least 21 but less than 37 years of age at the time of appointment. You must pass a background investigation, an interview and be in excellent physical condition. You must have a bachelor's degree or three years of responsible experience. An equivalent combination of education and experience will also meet the requirements.

Training

Deportation Officers attend nine weeks of training at the Federal Law Enforcement Training Center in Glynco, Georgia. Officers study Immigration laws, escort and transportation of detainees, civil rights, constitutional law, Detention Enforcement Officer duties and responsibilities, behavioral science, defensive measures, arrest techniques, physical conditioning, use of firearms and the Spanish language.

Salary

Initial appointments are at grade GS-4 or GS-5 depending on the applicant's qualifications. Career progression is to the GS-7 level. Promotions to higher grades are made on a competitive basis.

How To Apply

You must establish an eligible rating with the Office of Personnel Management. This is done through either a written test or by filling out a questionnaire that reflects your previous experience.

For further information contact the Immigration and Naturalization Service, Personnel Division, 800 K Street, 5th Floor, Washington, D.C. 20536 or call (202) 514-2530, or visit their internet site at http://www.ins.usdoj.gov

National Marine Fisheries Service
Special Agent

The National Marine Fisheries Service (NMFS) is the compliance element of the National Oceanic and Atmospheric Administration (NOAA) and the only Federal agency dedicated full time to the protection and conservation of our nation's living marine resources. Special Agents are responsible for initiating and conducting full-scale investigations of alleged criminal and civil violations under the various fish and wildlife laws. This involves interrogating suspects and interviewing witnesses; conducting searches and seizures; making arrests; testifying in court; and carrying out undercover operations. Duties and responsibilities bring agents into frequent contact with foreign and domestic law enforcement officials, criminal elements, foreign nationals, all segments of the fishing industry, import/export brokers/dealers and smugglers in protected products, and the general public. Acts as liaison with other Federal, State, and local law enforcement agencies and cooperates with them during the investigation and prosecution.

Qualifications

Applicants must be a U. S. citizen and less than 37 years of age. They must have a four-year college degree or three years of law enforcement experience may be substituted for the educational requirements. They must be able to pass a background investigation and a comprehensive medical exam.

Training

New Agents will attend nine weeks of Criminal Investigator training at the Federal Law Enforcement Training Center. In addition, they will attend a four-week Marine Law Enforcement Training Program, and a four-week National Oceanic Atmospheric Administration Enforcement Basic Training Program. They will also receive seven weeks of Field Officer Training.

Salary

Initial appointments are generally made at the GS-5 or GS-7 level. Career progression to GS-9 and GS-11 generally follow at one year intervals. Opportunities for promotions to higher grades are on a competitive basis.

How To Apply
Submit an SF-171, or an Optional Form 612 or a resume to the National Marine Fisheries Office of Law Enforcement. If you are applying for a specific job opening, your paperwork should be submitted to the office where the vacancy exists. Vacancy announcements may be obtained from OPM or the NMFS.

For additional information, write to the National Marine Fisheries Office of Law Enforcement, 8484 Georgia Avenue, Suite 415, Silver Springs, DM 20910, or call them at (301) 427-2300, or visit their web site at http://www.nmfs.noaa.gov/ole/fen.html

Bureau of Indian Affairs Criminal Investigator

Located throughout the United States are Indian reservations and Indian owned lands. These lands are governed by Tribal law. The U.S. Department of the Interior, Bureau of Indian Affairs has Criminal Investigators who investigate Federal crimes, make arrests for such crimes and assist in the prosecution of those crimes committed on Indian lands within the BIA's jurisdiction. BIA Criminal Investigators work with other law enforcement agencies who may be seeking individuals living on Indian lands. When filling vacancies in the BIA, priority in selection will be given to qualified Indian candidates.

Qualifications
You must be at least 21 years old and not more than 35 years old. You must have completed four years of study at a college or university or have three years of general experience and one year of specialized experience. You must pass a background investigation, an oral interview and a physical examination.

Training
Selected applicants attend a nine-week Criminal Investigator Course at the Federal Law Enforcement Training Center in Glynco, Georgia.

Salary
Criminal Investigators begin at a GS-5, GS-7 or GS-9 grade level depending on one's qualifications. The journeyman grade is a GS-11. Opportunities exist for promotions to higher grade levels.

How To Apply
If you qualify under the Indian Preference Act, you may apply directly to the BIA for any current openings. BIA generally hires Federal employees transferring from another agency. Occasionally, OPM will give a written test to establish a list from which BIA will hire Criminal Investigators.

For further information call the BIA's Personnel Office at (202) 208-3711. You can also write to the Bureau of Indian Affairs, Office of Public Affairs, 1849 C Street, NW, Washington, D.C. 20240, or visit their internet site at http://www.doi.gov/bureau-indian-affairs.html

Bureau of Indian Affairs Federal Police Officer

This position is under the U.S. Department of Interior, Bureau of Indian Affairs, Office of Law Enforcement Services. Federal Police Officers enforce the laws in the Indian Country. They investigate crimes and make arrest for crimes committed on Indian lands within the BIA's jurisdiction.

Qualifications
You must be between the ages of 21 and 37 and possess a high school diploma or GED equivalent. You must be in excellent physical condition. You must pass an interview, medical examination and a background investigation. Priority will be given

to Indian candidates. However, all candidates will receive consideration without regard to race, color, sex, religion, national origin or other non-merit factors.

Training
Trainees receive approximately eight weeks of training in basic law enforcement techniques at the Federal Law Enforcement Training Center in Glynco, Georgia.

Salary
Initial appointments are made at a grade GS-5 grade level with opportunities to advance to the higher grade levels. Depending on your qualifications, you may be able to start at a GS-7, GS-9 or higher grade.

How To Apply
To obtain a vacancy announcement, contact the Office of Law Enforcement Services at (505) 248-7937.

For further information write to the Bureau of Indian Affairs, Office of Public Affairs, 1849 C Street, NW, Washington, D.C. 20240, or call the BIA's Personnel Office at (202) 208-3711, or visit their internet site at http://www.doi.gov/bureau-indian-affairs.html

United States Air Force Special Investigations Criminal Investigator

Civilian criminal investigators plan and conduct criminal investigations of suspected violations of the uniform code of military justice and/or criminal laws of the United States affecting the conduct and integrity of Air Force personnel. They interview witnesses, examine records, prepare written reports, perform undercover assignments and testify in court-martial hearings. This is a civilian position.

Qualifications

A bachelor's degree from an accredited college meets the minimal educational requirements. An applicant who possesses experience in conducting investigations and has knowledge of Federal statutes and the rules of evidence may be accepted. Applicants may be required to pass a polygraph examination and must be eligible for top secret clearance. Applicants must be available for reassignment to another duty station anyplace in the word where Air Force units are stationed. Active duty members must be within 120 days of their established separate date by closing date of the job announcement.

Training

Selected applicants attend a 11-week AFOSI criminal investigator course at the U.S. Air Force Special Investigations Academy at Andrews AFB, MD. Candidates must also demonstrate proficiency in the use of firearms according to AFOSI standards.

Salary

Initial appointments are generally made at the GS-11 level. Opportunities exist for promotion to a grade GS-12 on a competitive basis.

How To Apply

Write to AFOSI and request a copy of any vacancy announcements they currently have open. Submit a completed SF-171. If applicable, submit proof of veterans' preference (DD Form 214).

For further information write to the AFOSI/DPC, 1535 Command Drive, Suite CD-204, Andrews AFB, MD 20762-7002, or call their Personnel Office at (240) 857-2166 / 2182 / 2183, or visit their internet site at http://www.dtic.mil/afosi

United States Capitol Police
Police Officer

The U.S. Capitol Police was established in 1828. The U.S. Capitol Police provide law enforcement and investigative services within the Capitol, House and Senate Office Buildings, and adjoining streets and parks, to Members of Congress and the Congressional community. The U.S. Capitol Police have several specialized units which enhance the performance of their duties. The Containment and Emergency Response Team (CERT) is a well-trained unit capable of countering an armed assault upon the Congress. The Threat Assessment Unit conducts inquiries into all threats against Members of Congress. If necessary, the Protective Operations Section will provide 24 hour protection to the Congressional Member anywhere in the United States. Other specialized units are: the K-9 Explosive Detection Section, Patrol Division, Criminal Investigation Division, and Electronic Countermeasures Section.

Qualifications
Applicants must be U.S. citizens between the ages of 21 and 37. You must have a high school diploma or equivalent. You will be required to pass a written exam, an interview, a polygraph test, a psychological test, a background investigation and a medical exam. Vision must be at least 20/100 uncorrected and correctable to 20/20.

Training
Training begins with a two-week orientation at the Capitol Police training facility in Washington, D.C. followed by an eight-week Police Training Course at the Federal Law Enforcement Training Center in Glynco, Georgia. Recruits then return to the Capitol Police Training Division for an additional ten weeks of comprehensive training prior to assignment.

Salary
The U.S. Capitol Police has its own pay scale. Candidates start at around $35,000 per year. Upon successful completion of all training requirements, officers then receive a salary of around

$37,000. Opportunities for promotions are available on a competitive basis.

How To Apply

Write or call the Capitol Police to obtain the next date for the written examination. The examination is administered at the Capitol Police Headquarters in Washington, D.C. Those applicants who pass the written test are given an application and information necessary for further processing.

For further information contact the U.S. Capitol Police, Public Information Office, 119 D Street N.E., Washington, D.C. 20510-7218, or call their job hotline at (202) 224-9819, or visit the web site http://www.usajobs.opm.gov

Defense Criminal Investigative Service Special Agent

This is a civilian position with the Office of the Inspector General (OIG). The OIG is responsible for the prevention and detection of fraud, waste and abuse in the programs and operations of the Department of Defense. The Assistant Inspector General for Investigations is responsible for investigations of the OIG and DoD. The primary mission of the Special Agent is to investigate white collar crimes with a secondary mission to investigate general crimes.

Qualifications

Three years of responsible general experience plus one year of criminal investigative experience meets the requirements for a GS-7 level position. There are some substitutions for education. You must be under the age of 37 at the time your application is received in the DoD Personnel Office. You must pass a physical examination, a background investigation and a drug test. You must have uncorrected vision of no less than 20/200, correctable to 20/20 in one eye, and 20/40 in the other eye.

Training
Special Agents receive approximately fifteen weeks of criminal investigative training at the Federal Law Enforcement Training Center in Glynco, Georgia.

Salary
Initial appointments are made at the GS-7 to GS-12 level depending on the amount of experience and education. There is a possible promotion potential to a grade GS-13.

How To Apply
Complete an SF-171 and mail it to the Office of the Inspector General, Department of Defense, Personnel and Security Directorate, Attn: Team A, Personnel Operations Division, Supply File, 400 Army Navy Drive, Arlington VA 22202-2884. Desired geographical locations and lowest acceptable grades should be specified on the application. When there are vacancies, applicants will be provided with instructions and a copy of the job announcement. The applications are retained for six months from date of receipt.

For further information contact the Inspector General, Department of Defense, Personnel Division, 400 Army Navy Drive, Arlington VA 22202-2884 or call their personnel office at (703) 604-9730, or visit their internet site at http://www.dodig.osd.mil/DCIS/dcismain.html

United States Supreme Court Police Officer

The Supreme Court Police work in the Washington, D.C. area protecting the Supreme Court Building and grounds, the Supreme Court Justices and other personnel located in the Supreme Court Building.

Qualifications
Prior police or security experience with a thorough knowledge of law enforcement techniques is desired. A four-year college degree may be substituted for experience. You must pass an interview before a police panel, a medical examination and a background investigation. There is no 37-year age limitation.

Training
Selected applicants undergo an eight-week Police Training Course conducted at the Federal Law Enforcement Training Center in Glynco, Georgia. Applicants also receive training specific to their duties.

Salary
Supreme Court Police Officers have their own pay scale. Candidates start at around $32,000 per year. After six months of successful job performance, they receive a salary of about $34,000 per year. There are annual opportunities for increases.

How To Apply
Being an exempt agency not governed by the Office of Personnel Management, you apply directly to the Supreme Court Police by completing an SF-171. If selected for an interview, travel to Washington, D.C. will be at the applicant's expense. There is no written test.

For further information contact the U.S. Supreme Court, Personnel Office, Room 3, One First Street N.E., Washington, D.C. 20543 or call their personnel office at (202) 479-3404.

Federal Protection Service
Federal Protective Officer

The Federal Protective Service is the security arm of the U.S. General Services Administration, the agency responsible for most civilian work space owned or leased by the Federal Government. It is the FPS's job to protect the Federal workplace and ensure the safety of employees and visitors nationwide. FPS consists of a mobile police of uniformed Federal Protective Officers (FPO's). These officers are authorized to enforce laws and make arrests on property under the control of the U.S. General Services Administration (GSA).

An additional force of non-uniformed criminal investigators examines crimes ranging from theft of Government property to homicide. Investigators coordinate their efforts with other law enforcement agencies.

Qualifications
You must have a high school diploma and one year of police experience or an appropriate amount of college education. You must pass a physical examination, a drug test and a background investigation. You must be at least 21 years of age.

Training
Selected applicants attend an eight-week Police Training Course conducted at the Federal Law Enforcement Training Center in Glynco, Georgia. Officers also receive specialized training in crowd and riot control and in performing police functions with national security significance.

Salary
Federal Protective Officers start at a grade GS-4/5/6 depending on one's qualifications and geographical area. They receive annual step increases over a three-year period. Opportunities for promotions are on a competitive basis.

How To Apply
You must establish an eligibility rating by taking the appropriate written test administered by the Office of Personnel Management. FPS is current hiring in only large metropolitan areas. Vacancy announcements may be obtained either through OPM or the GSA Human Resources Division.

For further information contact the nearest FPS office or write to the Federal Protective Service, Room 2341, 1800 F Street N.W., Washington, D.C. 20405, or call their personnel office at (202) 501-0907, or visit their web site at http://hydra.gsa.gov/pbs/fps

Contact Information for 70 Other Federal Law Enforcement Agencies

DEPARTMENT OF DEFENSE

DEFENSE INTELLIGENCE AGENCY

Special Agents with the DIA are the primary managers and producers of foreign military intelligence. They are also involved with drug interdiction.

For more information contact:
Defense Intelligence Agency
Civilian Personnel Division (DAH-2)
Washington, D.C. 20340-5100
(703) 907-1710 or 800 526-4629

SECURITY OF DEFENSE

Department of Defense Police Officers maintain law and order in and around DOD buildings. They check passes, regulate traffic and conduct criminal investigations such as robbery, assault and theft.

For more information contact:
Department of Defense
Washington Headquarters Services
Washington, D.C. 20301-1155
(703) 695-4249

DEFENSE INVESTIGATIVE SERVICES

Special Agents with DIS conduct security investigations on personnel within the Department of Defense to ensure that all employees are of the highest integrity.

For more information contact:
Defense Investigative Service
Public Affairs Office
1900 Half Street, SW
Washington, S.C. 20324-1700
(202) 475-1062

DEPARTMENT OF LABOR

OCCUPATIONAL SAFETY AND HEALTH ADMINISTRATION

By conducting inspections in the workplace, Inspectors with OSHA prevent injuries and protect the health of the American worker by enforcing the various health and job safety standards.

For more information contact:
Occupational Safety and Health Administration
820 First Street, NE, Suite 440
Washington, D.C. 20002
(202) 523-1452

EMPLOYMENT STANDARDS ADMINISTRATION

Investigators with ESA enforce the laws governing legally-mandated wages and working conditions, including child labor, minimum wages, overtime and family and medical leave.

For more information contact:
Employment Standards Administration
U.S. Department of Labor
Office of Public Affairs
200 Constitution Avenue, NW, Room S-1032
Washington, D.C. 20210
(202) 219-8211

MINE SAFETY AND HEALTH ADMINISTRATION

Investigators with MSHA enforce the mandatory safety standards to eliminate fatal accidents, reduce the frequency of accidents and to minimize health hazards in the Nation's mines.

For more information contact:
Mine Safety and Health Administration
Office of Information Public Affairs
4015 Wilson Boulevard, Room 601
Arlington, VA 22230
(703) 235-1452

PENSION AND WELFARE BENEFITS ADMINISTRATION

Investigators with PWBA protect the integrity of pensions, health care plans, welfare plans and other employee benefits. They convict violators of the relevant statutes.

For more information contact:
Pension and Welfare Benefits Administration
U.S. Department of Labor
200 Constitution Avenue, NW
Washington, D.C. 20210
(202) 219-6471

DEPARTMENT OF COMMERCE

OFFICE OF EXPORT ENFORCEMENT

Criminal Investigators with the OEE enforce the export control laws by executing search warrants, seizing goods about to be shipped illegally and by making arrests.

For more information contact:
Office of Export Enforcement
U.S. Department of Commerce
14th and Constitution Avenue, NW, Room 4616
Washington, D.C. 20230
(202) 482-2252

OTHER MISCELLANEOUS AGENCIES

NATIONAL SECURITY AGENCY

Agents with the NSA work in the intelligence community. They intercept and analyze foreign communications of all types.

For more information contact:
National Security Agency
Employment Office
Attn: M3221 (AIL)

Fort George G Meade, MD 20755-6000
(301) 688-6524

TENNESSEE VALLEY AUTHORITY

The TVA is the Nation's largest power corporation. TVA police officers protect TVA buildings, property and personnel.

For more information contact:
Tennessee Valley Authority
400 West Summit Hill Drive
Knoxville, TN 37902-1499
(615) 632-8489

SECURITIES AND EXCHANGE COMMISSION

The enforcement staff conducts investigations into possible violations of the federal securities laws by examining brokers, investment advisors and security dealers.

For more information contact:
Securities and Exchange Commission
Division of Enforcement
450 Fifth Street, NW
Washington, D.C. 20545
(202) 942-4150

AMTRAK POLICE DEPARTMENT

Amtrak Police Officers protect employees, passengers and property and prevent and investigate criminal activity on board all Amtrak trains.

For more information contact:
Amtrak Police Department
30th Street Station, North Tower
Philadelphia, PA 19104
(215) 349-1245

LIBRARY OF CONGRESS

Library of Congress Police Officers serve in the Library's various buildings. They monitor alarm systems, subdue unruly persons and conduct inspections to detect any unsafe conditions.

For more information contact:
Library of Congress
Employment Office
101 Independence Avenue, SE
Washington, D.C. 20540
(202) 707-5627

UNITED STATES COAST GUARD
Working with other law enforcement agencies, the USCG enforces maritime laws and maritime safety.

For more information contact:
U.S. Coast Guard Recruiting Center
4200 Wilson Blvd., Suite 450
Arlington, VA 22202
800 424-8883 or 800 GET-USCG

UNITED STATES GENERAL ACCOUNTING OFFICE
Investigators with GAO's Office of Special Investigations are charged with detecting fraud and abuse within federally funded programs.

For more information contact:
U.S. General Accounting Office
441 G Street, NW
Washington, D.C. 20548
(202) 512-4800

NATIONAL ZOOLOGICAL PARK
The Park Police for the National Zoological Park enforce the rules and regulations, prevent crime and make arrests within the Zoological Park.

For more information contact:
National Zoological Park
3000 Connecticut Avenue, NW
Washington, D.C. 20008
(202) 673-4718

UNITED STATES GOVERNMENT PRINTING OFFICE
USGPO Police Officers maintain the law at U.S. Government Printing Offices facilities. They do this through patrols, standing guard and escorting classified national defense security information.

For more information contact:
U.S. Government Printing Office
Employment Branch, Room C-106
North Capitol and H Streets, NW
Washington, D.C. 20401
(202) 512-1187

NATIONAL INSTITUTE OF HEALTH
Police Officers with the NIH enforce the laws at NIH facilities and protect NIH employees.

For more information contact:
National Institute of Health
Police Branch
9000 Rockville Pike
Bethesda, MD 20892
(301) 496-1766

ENVIRONMENTAL PROTECTION AGENCY
Criminal Investigators with the EPA enforce the environment laws of the U.S. which are designed to control pollution.

For more information contact:
Environmental Protection Agency
Human Resources Office
401 M Street, SW
Washington, D.C. 20460
(202) 382-4361

OFFICE OF THE INSPECTOR GENERAL

The following departments have an Inspector General's Office which employs Criminal Investigators who are responsible for the prevention and detection of fraud, waste and abuse in the departmental operations and programs. They conduct audits, investigations and evaluations which help to improve the effectiveness, efficiency and economy of the department They also investigate complaints, allegations or other information indicating possible criminal activity or program abuse within the department. They work in cooperation with other federal law enforcement agencies and the U.S. Attorney's Office in prosecuting cases. For more information contact the agencies listed below.

SMALL BUSINESS ADMINISTRATION
Office of the Inspector General
409 3rd Street, SW
Washington, D.C. 20416
(202) 205-6586

UNITED STATES DEPARTMENT OF COMMERCE
Office of the Inspector General
Room 7713
14th & Constitution Avenue, NW
Washington, D.C. 20230
(202) 482-4661

DEPARTMENT OF TRANSPORTATION
Office of the Inspector General
400 7th Street, SW, Room 2440
Washington, D.C. 20590
(202) 366-8734

DEPARTMENT OF DEFENSE
Office of the Inspector General
400 Army Navy Drive
Arlington, VA 22202-2884
(703) 604-8300

DEPARTMENT OF HEALTH AND HUMAN SERVICES
Office of the Inspector General
200 Independence Avenue, SW
Washington, D.C. 20201
(202) 619-0257

DEPARTMENT OF AGRICULTURE
Office of the Inspector General
14th Street & Constitution Avenue, SW
Washington, D.C. 20250
(202) 720-2791

AMTRAK
Office of the Inspector General
400 North Capitol Street, NW
Washington, D.C. 20001
(202) 906-4600

INTERSTATE COMMERCE COMMISSION
Office of the Inspector General
12th Street & Constitution Avenue, NW
Washington, D.C. 20423
(202) 275-1763

GENERAL SERVICES ADMINISTRATION
Office of the Inspector General
18th & F Street, NW
Washington, D.C. 20405
(202) 501-0450

DEPARTMENT OF ENERGY
Office of the Inspector General
1000 Independence Avenue, SW
Washington, D.C. 20585
(202) 586-1924

RAILROAD RETIREMENT BOARD
Office of the Inspector General
844 North Rush Street
Chicago, IL 60611
(312) 751-4350

CORPORATION FOR PUBLIC BROADCASTING
Office of the Inspector General
901 E Street, NW
Washington, D.C. 20004
(202) 879-9660

GOVERNMENT PRINTING OFFICE
Office of the Inspector General
North Capitol& H Streets, NW
Washington, D.C. 20401
(202) 512-0039

TENNESSEE VALLEY AUTHORITY
Office of the Inspector General
400 West Summit Hill Drive
Knoxville, TN 37902
(423) 632-4120

DEPARTMENT OF EDUCATION
Office of the Inspector General
400 Independence Avenue, SW
Washington, D.C. 20202
(202) 205-5770

DEPARTMENT OF STATE
Office of the Inspector General
2201 C Street, NW, Room 6817
Washington, D.C. 20520
(202) 647-9450

NUCLEAR REGULATORY COMMISSION
Office of the Inspector General
Mail Stop T5 D28
Washington, D.C. 20555
(301) 415-5930

BOARD FOR INTERNATIONAL BROADCASTING
Office of the Inspector General
1201 Connecticut Avenue, NW
Washington, D.C. 20036
(202) 254-8040

FEDERAL MARITIME COMMISSION
Office of the Inspector General
800 North Capitol Street, NW, Room 1072
Washington, D.C. 20573
(202) 523-5863

NATIONAL LABOR RELATIONS BOARD
Office of the Inspector General
1099 14th Street, NW, Room 5820
Washington, D.C. 20570
(202) 273-1960

U.S. TRADE COMMISSION
Office of the Inspector General
500 E Street, SW
Washington, D.C. 20436
(202) 252-2210

DEPARTMENT OF HOUSING AND URBAN DEVELOPMENT
Office of the Inspector General
451 7th Street, SW
Washington, D.C. 20410
(202) 708-0430

ENVIRONMENTAL PROTECTION AGENCY
Office of the Inspector General
401 M Street, SW, (2441)
Washington, D.C. 20460
(202) 260-3177

APPALACHIAN REGIONAL COMMISSION
Office of the Inspector General
1666 Connecticut Avenue, NW, Suite 215
Washington, D.C. 20235
(202) 884-7625

FEDERAL DEPOSIT INSURANCE CORPORATION
Office of the Inspector General
801 17th Street, NW, Room 1096
Washington, D.C. 20434
(202) 416-2026

FEDERAL TRADE COMMISSION
Office of the Inspector General
6th Street & Pennsylvania Avenue, NW
Washington, D.C. 20580

(202) 326-2800

PEACE CORPS
Office of the Inspector General
1990 K Street, NW, Room 5302
Washington, D.C. 20526
(202) 606-3320

DEPARTMENT OF THE INTERIOR
Office of the Inspector General
1849 C Street, NW
Washington, D.C. 20240
(202) 208-4356

NATIONAL AERONAUTICS AND SPACE ADMINISTRATION
Office of the Inspector General
300 E Street, SW, Code W, Room 8V69
Washington, D.C. 20546
(202) 358-1220

CONSUMER PRODUCT SAFETY COMMISSION
Office of the Inspector General
4330 East West Highway
Bethesda, MD 20814
(301) 504-0573

FEDERAL LABOR RELATIONS AUTHORITY
Office of the Inspector General
607 14th Street, NW
Washington, D.C. 20424
(202) 482-6570

NATIONAL CREDIT UNION ADMINISTRATION
Office of the Inspector General
1775 Duke Street
Alexandria, VA 22314-3428
(703) 518-6350

NATIONAL SCIENCE FOUNDATION
Office of the Inspector General

4201 Wilson Blvd., Room 1135
Alexandria, VA 22230
(703) 306-2100

DEPARTMENT OF JUSTICE
Office of the Inspector General
10th Street & Constitution Avenue, NW, Suite 4206
Washington, D.C. 20530
(202) 514-3435

FEDERAL EMERGENCY MANAGEMENT AGENCY
Office of the Inspector General
500 C Street, SW, Room 505
Washington, D.C. 20472
(202) 646-3910

BOARD OF GOVERNORS OF THE FEDERAL RESERVE SYSTEM
Office of the Inspector General
20TH Street & Constitution Avenue, NW
Washington, D.C. 20551
(202) 862-3800

FEDERAL COMMUNICATIONS COMMISSION
Office of the Inspector General
1919 M Street, NW, Room 752
Washington, D.C. 20554
(202) 418-0420

SECURITY AND EXCHANGE COMMISSION
Office of the Inspector General
450 5TH Street, NW
Washington, D.C. 20549
(202) 942-4461

DEPARTMENT OF THE TREASURY
Office of the Inspector General
1500 Pennsylvania Avenue, NW, Room 2412
Washington, D.C. 20220
(202) 622-1090

COMMODITY FUTURES TRADING COMMISSION
Office of the Inspector General
1155 21st Street, NW
Washington, D.C. 20581
(202) 418-5110

FEDERAL ELECTION COMMISSION
Office of the Inspector General
999 E Street, NW, Room 940
Washington, D.C. 20463
(202) 219-4267

NATIONAL ENDOWMENT FOR THE HUMANITIES
Office of the Inspector General
1100 Pennsylvania Avenue, NW, Room 419
Washington, D.C. 20506
(202) 606-8350

SMITHSONIAN INSTITUTION
Office of the Inspector General
955 L'Enfant Plaza, SW, Room 7600
Washington, D.C. 20560
(202) 287-3326

DEPARTMENT OF VETERANS AFFAIRS
Office of the Inspector General
810 Vermont Avenue, NW
Washington, D.C. 20420
(202) 565-8620

U.S. INFORMATION AGENCY
Office of the Inspector General
400 6th Street, SW
Washington, D.C. 05472
(202) 401-7202

EQUAL EMPLOYMENT OPPORTUNITY COMMISSION
Office of the Inspector General
1801 L Street, NW, Suite 3001
Washington, D.C. 20507
(202) 663-4379

DEPARTMENT OF LABOR
Office of the Inspector General
200 Constitution Avenue, NW, Room S-5508
Washington, D.C. 20210
(202) 219-6730

FARM CREDIT ADMINISTRATION
Office of the Inspector General
1501 Farm Credit Drive
McLean, VA 22102
(703) 883-4030

NATIONAL ENDOWMENT FOR THE ARTS
Office of the Inspector General
1100 Pennsylvania Avenue, NW
Washington, D.C. 20506
(202) 682-5402

NATIONAL ARCHIVES AND RECORDS ADMINISTRATION
Office of the Inspector General
8601 Adelphi Road, Room 1300
College Park, MD 20740
(301) 713-6666

AGENCY OF INTERNATIONAL DEVELOPMENT
Office of the Inspector General
320 21st Street, NW
Washington, D.C. 20523
(202) 647-7844

Chapter II
Federal Law Enforcement Entrance Test

Federal Law Enforcement Entrance Test

Most federal law enforcement agencies have a written entrance examination that an applicant must pass in order to be considered for employment. Some agencies administer their own test and they maintain a roster of passing scores. For the majority of the federal agencies, the Office of Personnel Management (OPM) will administer the written entrance test. OPM and not the agencies maintains a list of the scores. When an agency is hiring, OPM will provide the agency with a list of the highest passing scores. This system is designed to prevent any nepotism. Once an agency has exhausted the list, if they continue to hire off the same test, OPM will then provide them with the lower passing scores. Therefore, the higher you score on the entrance test, the sooner you will move onto the next phase of the hiring process which is usually the oral interview.

While there are several different types of tests that you can take, the biggest and probably the hardest is the Treasury Enforcement Agent (TEA) examination. The TEA is the test given for most of the Treasury jobs. This includes Special Agent careers with the U.S. Secret Service, the Bureau of Alcohol, Tobacco and Firearms, the Internal Revenue Service and the U.S. Customs Service. By passing this one test, you establish a rating for all of these agencies. In 1997, the U.S. Marshals Service patterned their test around the TEA examination.

This guide will help prepare you for the TEA and the USMS test as well as other federal law enforcement tests. While the various exams will differ, they all test you on your reasoning abilities. The test usually has three sections: verbal skills, mathematical skills and investigative skills. The exam is usually timed. You have approximately 45 to 60 minutes to complete one section of the test consisting of 15 to 25 questions. There are three sections as mentioned above. You have plenty of time so read the questions carefully. If you get stuck on a difficult question, skip over it and move onto the remaining questions. Once you have finished answering the remaining questions go back to any questions that you skipped.

With the exception of a possible essay question to grade your writing skills, all of the questions will be multiple choice. Read the question and see if you can figure out the answer before looking at the choices. You will record your answers on an answer sheet by filling in an oval that corresponds to the correct answer. Be sure to fill in the answer space completely. If you change an answer, be sure to erase it completely.

Grading is done by counting how many questions you answered correctly. Therefore, you should answer **all** of the questions. If you are uncertain of the correct answer, make a selection with an educated guess.

If time permits, after finishing a section of the test go back and review your answers. Remember that your first selection is usually the correct answer. Therefore, you should not change your answer unless you know for sure that you initially selected the wrong answer. Check to see that you have answered every question. Make certain that your answers have been properly recorded.

We have included sample questions covering the three areas usually found on the test: verbal skills, mathematical skills and investigative skills. Read the sample questions and answers carefully. Record your answers on a sheet of paper. You can then compare your answers with the correct answers which are listed at the end of the chapter. We have also provided an explanation as to why one answer is correct and the other answers are incorrect.

Federal Law Enforcement Sample Test Questions

Verbal Reasoning Questions

In this part of the test you will be given a paragraph that contains certain information. After you read the paragraph, you will be asked a question concerning the information that was provided. In answering the question, use only the information that was given to you. Do not base your answers on any previous knowledge that you may have about the subject matter but consider only the information listed in the paragraph. Some paragraphs will be written in such a way that they may appear to be repetitious and somewhat confusing. Reread the paragraph several times if necessary and try to identify the important aspects of the information. They are testing you to see if you understand what you have read. They are trying to determine if you have the ability to discern the information and recognize a reasonable answer. Read the paragraph carefully. The questions on the test will be much more difficult than the sample questions listed below.

Verbal Reasoning Sample Questions:

1. A government vehicle is to be used for official business. The employee must be performing his duties when driving the vehicle. The employee need not be "on duty" so long as the use of the vehicle is for government business. An employee may use a government vehicle for personal business if he is "on duty" and making a stop that is not out of his direction of official travel.

Which of the following statements is best supported by this paragraph?

A. A government vehicle may be used for personal matters if the employee is not working and does not deviate from his route of travel.

B. A government employee who is "off duty" may not drive a government vehicle for personal business or official business.

C. Using a government vehicle for strictly personal matters is prohibited.

D. An "on duty" government employee may only use a government vehicle to perform his duties as a government official.

E. When driving a government vehicle, an employee need not be "on duty" or performing any kind of working assignment.

2. When conducting a fugitive investigation an investigator can use many different sources of information. The more information that an investigator has the easier it will be to locate the fugitive. Most of the information that an investigator needs may be obtained by interviewing the fugitive's associates. The information obtained from the fugitive's friends and relatives may lead to where he is hiding. Other sources of information such as a driver's license or social security number may help an investigator to determine what alias the fugitive is using. The mail delivered by the Postal Service and telephone records may disclose the fugitive's location. Every source of information that the investigator has access to should be obtained.

Which of the following statements is best supported by this paragraph?

A. Computer checks on a driver's license, telephone records or social security number should be used if the investigator cannot locate the fugitive by other means.

B. An investigator who conducts a thorough interview of the fugitive's friends and family members will be able to identify the fugitive's whereabouts.

C. Because a court order is needed to view any mail delivered by the Postal Service, an investigator should use this resource as a last resort.

D. The best source of information for obtaining any aliases that the fugitive may be using is a driver's license inquiry or a review of the fugitive's social security number.

E. The key to any fugitive investigation is for the investigator to utilize all the informational resources available.

Investigative Questions

In this section of the test, you will be given a paragraph which describes an incident or problematic situation. Following the paragraph will be up to ten witness statements that were taken during the investigation. After reading the paragraph and the witness statements, you will have to answer several questions concerning the witness statements as they pertain to the investigation. Carefully read the witness statements. You should ask yourself if these statements are based on fact or is the person giving their opinion as to what happened. Read the answers and compare them to each other to see which statement answers the question.

Investigative Sample Question A:

On August 2, 1996, an Illinois State Trooper made a traffic stop on a blue Dodge Caravan that was owned and driven by Thomas Davis. Traveling in the van with Davis was Jim Barnes. The Trooper observed a small amount of cocaine in the van and arrested both individuals for possession of cocaine. On August 29, 1996, Davis and Barnes pled guilty to the charges. Davis was placed on probation for two years and Barnes was sentenced to serve two years at a prison camp in Terre Haute, Indiana. After serving six months of his sentence, Barnes was assigned to work the maintenance detail which allowed him to work outside with minimal supervision. On May 22, 1997, the prison conducted its usual head count at 10:00 p.m. At that time, it was discovered that Jim Barnes was no longer at the institution and he was declared as an escapee. On May 25, 1997, Jim Barnes was arrested by the U.S. Marshals in Springfield, Illinois.

An investigation by the U.S. Marshals Service as to how Jim Barnes was able to escape and if he received any assistance in escaping yielded the following statements:

1. Correctional Officer Bob James stated that on May 22 he assigned Jim Barnes along with five other inmates to trim some trees located behind the prison camp. James recalled

seeing Barnes still working at around 4:30 p.m. At 5:00 p.m. when they stopped working, several inmates told Officer James that Barnes had entered the prison building to use the bathroom.

2. Thomas Davis who resides at 512 Sandgate, Springfield, Illinois stated that he has known Jim Barnes since childhood. Davis said he has written to and telephoned Barnes numerous times since his incarceration.

3. Correctional Officer Troy Thompson stated that on May 22 at around 4:45 p.m. inmate Jim Barnes entered the prison complex and said that he was quitting early because he was not feeling well. He allowed Barnes to go to his cell unescorted.

4. Deputy U.S. Marshal Ed McGrath stated that while searching Barnes cell he found a letter Barnes had received from an unknown individual. In the letter was the phrase, "May 22 is good." The letter was postmarked May 15, 1997, Springfield, Illinois.

5. Inmate David Jones stated that he was working with Barnes on May 22. Sometime after 4:30 p.m. Barnes told him he was going inside to use the facilities. That was the last time he saw Barnes.

6. Shirley Kerns who is a neighbor of Thomas Davis stated that Davis usually drives his truck everywhere he goes and rarely drives his van. The van has been sitting in front of his house for approximately four months without being driven. She believes the van is not running.

7. Deputy U.S. Marshal Jeff Sharkey stated that when he arrested Barnes, Barnes peacefully surrendered.

8. Correctional Officer Daryl Jennings stated that around 5:05 p.m. on May 22, 1997 he saw a blue van driving down the access road located behind the prison camp. Jennings could not tell who was in the van.

9. Inmate Jerry Hines stated that at around 6:30 p.m. he asked Correctional Officer Thompson if Barnes was ok. Officer Thompson told him that Barnes was feeling better.

10. Robert Cowens who is a neighbor of Thomas Davis stated that on May 22, 1997 at around 10:00 p.m. he observed two men entering Davis's house.

A-1. Which two statements indicate that Thomas Davis may have assisted Jim Barnes in escaping?

A. Statements 2 and 4

B. Statements 2 and 6

C. Statements 4 and 10

D. Statements 4 and 8

E. Statements 8 and 10

A-2. Which statement would best help Davis in his claim that he did not help Barnes escape?

A. Statement 2

B. Statement 4

C. Statement 6

D. Statement 8

E. Statement 10

A-3. Which statement best indicates that a correctional officer may have been involved in Barnes's escape?

A. Statement 1

B. Statement 3

C. Statement 4

D. Statement 8

E. Statement 9

A-4. Which statement has no direct importance in the investigation?

A. Statement 1

B. Statement 2

C. Statement 6

D. Statement 7

E. Statement 10

Investigative Sample Question B:
Judge Roy Min is a U.S. District Judge in Cleveland, Ohio. From November 1 - 10, 1996, he was the presiding judge at the trial of John Barker. Barker is a member of a radical anti-government group called *The People*. The group which is suspected in carrying out terrorist acts has a headquarters at 533 4th Street, Cleveland, Ohio. On November 10, 1996, Barker was convicted of attempting to murder an FBI agent. Two months after Barker's conviction, a package was mailed to Judge Min at his office in the Federal Courthouse. The package looked suspicious to the judge so he turned it over to the Bureau of Alcohol, Tobacco and Firearms. ATF discovered that the package contained a bomb and they safely detonated it.

An investigation by the FBI for attempted murder of a federal judge produced the following statements:

1. Judge Min stated that the package he received was handwritten, had no return address and had a postmark of Cleveland, Ohio.

2. A confidential informant stated that Ron Springs told him that *People* member Jerry Stack told him, "That judge and the rest of those pigs will pay for this injustice."

3. Gerald Cox the prosecuting U.S. Attorney stated that he observed the following *People* members attending the trial: Greg Simmons, Jerry Stack, Vanessa Darby and Kim Combs.

4. ATF Agent Robert Sloan stated that the package contained a metal pipe bomb that was filled with black powder and had approximately 40 nails attached to it.

5. Dan Fortney, a former member of *The People* group stated that one week after Barker's conviction Vanessa Darby asked him for the address to the Federal Courthouse in Cleveland.

6. A handwriting expert stated that the writing on the package sent Judge Min was written by a male.

7. Janice Kerns stated that her granddaughter Kim Combs was living with her in Miami, Florida from September 14 - December 8, 1996.

8. An FBI fingerprint examiner stated that only Judge Min's fingerprints were found on the package.

9. Larry Ryan stated that the Jerry Stack arrived at his house in Tampa, Florida on New Years Day 1997. Stack stayed with Ryan for three weeks.

10. FBI Agent Leonard Musser stated that while executing a search warrant at 533 4th Street, Cleveland, Ohio a can of black powder was found in a closet.

B-1. Which two statements would serve as the best evidence in court in tying members of *The People* with the mailing of the pipe bomb?

A. Statements 1 and 7

B. Statements 2 and 6

C. Statements 2 and 5

D. Statements 3 and 5

E. Statements 4 and 10

B-2. Which statement is based on hearsay?

A. Statement 1

B. Statement 2

C. Statement 3

D. Statement 5

E. Statement 9

B-3. Which two statements contradict each other?

A. Statements 2 and 9

B. Statements 3 and 7

C. Statements 3 and 9

D. Statements 5 and 6

E. Statements 4 and 10

B-4. Which statement is an alibi proving that a certain individual did not mail the bomb to Judge Min?

A. Statement 5

B. Statement 6

C. Statement 7

D. Statement 8

E. Statement 9

Mathematical Questions

For most individuals, this is probably the hardest part of a written law enforcement test. Some people become very discouraged when they read what appears to be a complicated math problem. The truth is in order to solve these arithmetic questions you do not need a degree in mathematics. You can find the answer by doing some simple multiplication, division, subtraction and addition. You will also need an understanding of certain terms in order to score high on this section of the test.

Averaging is the result obtained by dividing a sum by the number of quantities added. For example the average of 2, 10, 12 is the sum of 24 divided by the quantity of 3 which equals 8.

When averaging two rates such as miles per hour the question may not state the length of the distance traveled. As long as the distances are the same, such as in a return trip, you need to make up a simple length in order to do your calculations.

Ratio is the relationship in numbers between two similar things. This can be expressed as a fraction such as 1/3 or by using a colon 1:3. Ratios are read inserting the word "to" as "1 to 3."

Taxation rate is a percentage that has to be paid which is based on a fixed ratio. In calculating tax rates it is sometimes helpful to change the tax rate percentage into a decimal. For example 25% = .25

Cross Multiplying can be used when you are working with fractions that equal each other but one fraction has a missing number. By multiplying the top numbers with the opposite bottom numbers you can determine the missing number.

The questions will be given to you as a numerical question or as a short statement of the facts involving numerical amounts. Read the questions carefully and think about what you need to do in order to determine the correct answer. In this portion of the test, the last answer to each question will be "none of these." This makes it difficult in guessing the correct answer. You must take the time to do some accurate calculations. You cannot use a calculator in figuring out the answers. You will be given scratch paper that you can use to do your calculations.

Mathematical Averaging Sample Questions:

1. An odometer on a squad car shows that the car has been driven a total of 735 miles during a one week period. What is the average number of miles the car was driven each day during that one week period?

   A. 105 miles

   B. 123 miles

   C. 147 miles

   D. 245 miles

   E. None of these

2. A hot air balloon has flown a distance of 2,400 miles in 25 days flying 12 hours each day. What is the average speed the balloon was traveling?

   A. 6 mph

   B. 7 mph

   C. 8 mph

   D. 9 mph

   E. None of these

3. The police chased a suspect vehicle for 150 miles traveling at a speed of 75 miles per hour. After apprehending the suspect, they made the same trip back to the police station at 50 miles per hour. What was the average speed the squad car was traveling for both trips?

A. 55 mph

B. 60 mph

C. 62.5 mph

D. 65 mph

E. None of these

4. A motorist leaves his home and drives his vehicle at a rate of 40 miles per hour. His vehicle breaks down and he walks the same route back to his house at a rate of 5 miles per hour. What is the average rate he was traveling for both trips?

A. 2.2

B. 4.5

C. 8.0

D. 8.8

E. None of these

Mathematical Ratio Sample Questions:

1. A Secret Service office has 10 male agents and 5 female agents. The ratio of male agents to the number of agents in the office is:

A. 15:10

B. 5:10

C. 10:5

D. 10:15

E. None of these

2 On the blue prints to the new courthouse, 1/4 inch equals 1 foot of actual length. The blue prints show the judge's bench as being a line 2 ½ inches long. How long is the actual length of the judge's bench?

A. 5 feet

B. 8 feet

C. 9 feet

D. 10 feet

E. None of these

3. The ratio of 12 to 30 is:

A. 12:15

B. 24:60

C. 6:15

D. 12:100

E. None of these

Mathematical Taxation Rate Sample Questions:

1. An agent just bought a new pair of handcuffs for $25.00. The sales tax is computed at a rate of 5%. What will be his total cost for the handcuffs?

A. $25.25

B. $25.50

C. $26.00

D. $26.25

E. None of these

2. The Agent's Benevolent Fund needs to raise $4,410. They are considering taxing the souvenir items sold through their mail order catalog. It is estimated that the mail order sales will be $147,000 this year. What tax rate will yield $4,410?

A. 1%

B. 2%

C. 3%

D. 4%

E. None of these

3. The tax rate on purchasing gasoline is 2%. If the total tax paid is $60, what is the total dollar amount of gasoline purchased?

A. $120

B. $3,000

C. $6,000

D. $12,000

E. None of these

Cross Multiplying Sample Questions:
When working with fractions, cross multiplying can often help you find the correct answer. For example, if the equation is:

$$\frac{1}{8} = \frac{2}{?}$$

you would cross multiply 1 x ? and 2 x 8 which gives you the answer of ? = 16. 1/8 = 2/16. You can also use this formula when dealing with letters instead of numbers.

$$\frac{A}{B} = \frac{500}{?}$$

Cross multiplying gives you A? = 500B. You can then determine what ? is by dividing 500B by A. The correct answer is:

$$? = \frac{500B}{A}$$

You can also use cross multiplying in figuring percentages. An easy one would be what is 10% of 50? You should know that the answer is 5 and cross multiplying gives you the same answer.

$$\frac{10}{100} = \frac{x}{50} \qquad 100x = 500 \qquad x = \frac{500}{100} \quad x=5$$

1. A new police car will travel M miles on G gallons of gasoline. How many gallons of gasoline will be needed to travel Z number of miles?

A.	B.	C.	D.
$\frac{MG}{Z}$	$\frac{MZ}{G}$	$\frac{GZ}{M}$	$\frac{Z}{GM}$

Other Questions

Some agencies that administer their own written entrance examination may include some additional test questions. These questions may be in the form of an essay question, or they may be designed to gain more information about your personality.

Essay Question

This is usually one question designed to test your writing skills. Your handwriting should be legible but more importantly they are looking to see if you can organize your thoughts and express them in writing. The question may be about something that you did such as your greatest achievement or they may present you with a situation asking how you would handle it.

Before you write anything, take some time to think about what you want to write. The key is to write grammatically correct sentences that flow together. Use paragraphs to express your various thoughts on the matter. Make sure that all of your sentences are complete sentences. Do not try to use ten dollar words. Your writing will look more impressive with your clarity rather than your vocabulary.

Experience Questions

This part of the test usually has around 50 or more multiple choice questions that focus on your achievements, experiences and attitudes. It is designed to give the agency a better understanding of whom you are. Many of the questions do not have a right or wrong answer. However, you should answer the questions truthfully because your answers are subject to verification. If you provide any false information, this could be grounds for not hiring you or for your dismissal after you have been hired.

Experience Sample Question:

1. Which one of the following characteristics would your peers say bothers you most in people you meet?

   A. Bragging

B. Shyness

C. Lack of initiative

D. Trying to get something for nothing

E. Being very competitive

Answers
To the Sample Questions

Verbal Reasoning Answer Question #1
The correct answer is *C*. The government vehicle can be used for personal matters but there are certain restrictions. The employee must be "on duty and making a stop that is not out of his direction of official travel." Therefore, to use a government vehicle for only personal reasons would be a violation of policy.

Answer *A* is incorrect. It is true that a government vehicle may be used for personal matters if the employee does not deviate from his route of travel. However, the employee must be "on duty." Answer *A* states that the employee is "not working."

Answer *B* is incorrect because the paragraph states that the employee "need not be on duty so long as the use of the vehicle is for government business." An off duty employee may drive the vehicle if he is performing some type of government business.

Answer *D* is incorrect because of the word "only." The answer is saying that the use of a vehicle outside the scope of employment is prohibited. The paragraph says that an on duty government employee "may use the vehicle for personal business" if the employee is working and he makes a stop that is along his route of travel.

Answer *E* is incorrect. When using a government vehicle "the employee need not be on duty." However, the employee "must be performing his duties." You cannot drive a government vehicle for the sole purpose of conducting personal business.

Verbal Reasoning Answer Question #2
The correct answer is *E*. There are numerous sources of information available to the investigator. It may only take one source to lead to the fugitive's apprehension. However, the paragraph states, "Every source of information that the investigator has access to should be obtained."

Answer *A* is incorrect. The paragraph states, "The more information that an investigator has the easier it will be to locate the fugitive." Therefore, an investigator should seek computer checks at the start of the investigation and not as a last resort.

Answer *B* is incorrect because according to the paragraph thorough interview of the friends and family members "may" lead to locating the fugitive.

Answer *C* is incorrect because no where does it state that a court order is needed to obtain the information. The information should not be obtained as a last resort since "every source of information ....should be obtained."

Answer *D* is incorrect because the paragraph does not state that these are the best sources for obtaining aliases. The paragraph says that driver's license and social security information "may help an investigator to determine what alias the fugitive is using."

Investigative Answer Question #A-1

The correct answer is D. Statement #4 ties Davis to the escape because of the "Springfield" postmark and the letter which said "May 22 is good." Statement #8 places the same type of vehicle owned by Davis at the scene of the crime.

Investigative Answer Question #A-2

The correct answer is C. It appears that Barnes may have escaped in a blue van similar to the one Davis owns. The neighbor will testify that Davis usually drives his truck and hasn't driven the van for four months.

Investigative Answer Question #A-3

The correct answer is E. Statement #3 raises suspicion since Officer Thompson let Barnes return to his cell unescorted. However, statement #9 shows us that more than an hour after Barnes had escaped Officer Thompson was telling people that Barnes was ok.

Investigative Answer Question #A-4

The correct answer is D. The fact that Barnes surrendered to the U.S. Marshals has no bearing on how he escaped or who helped him escape.

Investigative Answer Question #B-1
The correct answer is E. Statements #4 and #10 provide hard evidence. The bomb was made using black powder and black powder was found at "The People's" headquarters.

Investigative Answer Question #B-2
The correct answer is B. The informant is repeating what Ron Springs told him. The confidential informant did not hear for himself what Jerry Stack said.

Investigative Answer Question #B-3
The correct answer is B. Gerald Cox stated that he saw Kim Combs attending the Barker's trail which was held November 1 - 8, 1997 in Cleveland. However, Janice Kerns has stated that Combs was with her in Miami during this same time period.

Investigative Answer Question #B-4
The correct answer is E. The mail bomb was placed in a mailbox in Cleveland two months after Barker's conviction on November 10, 1996. This means the bomb was mailed sometime close to January 10, 1997. Larry Ryan stated that Jerry Stack arrived at his house in Tampa on January 1, 1997 and stayed with him until approximately January 21, 1997. Therefore, Stack could not have mailed the bomb.

Mathematical Averaging Answer Question #1
The correct answer is A. In calculating the average, you divide the sum by the number of quantities. The sum is 735 and the quantity is 7 days in the week. 735 ÷ 7 = 105.

Mathematical Averaging Answer Question #2
The correct answer is C. 2,400 (the sum) divided by 25 (the quantity) = 96. You now know that the balloon traveled an average of 96 miles each day. In order to figure the average speed you take the sum of 96 miles and divide it by the quantity of 12 hours per day. 96 ÷ 12 = 8.

Mathematical Averaging Answer Question #3

The correct answer is B. The sum of 150 miles divided by the quantity of 75 mph equals 2 hours. The sum of 150 miles divided by the quantity of 50 mph equals 3 hours. The total sum of the trip is 300 miles divided by the total quantity time of 5 hours equals 60 mph.

Mathematical Averaging Answer Question #4

The correct answer is D. Since the distance traveled is not given you must make up a distance that is easy to calculate. Assume that the vehicle traveled 40 miles before breaking down. The calculations for the car are then 40 miles (sum) divided by 40 mph (quantity) equals 1. The calculation on walking would be 40 miles (sum) divided by 5 mph (quantity) equals 8. The total distance traveled is 80 miles divided by 9 the total time spent traveling equals 8.8 the average rate for both trips.

Mathematical Ratio Answer Question #1

The correct answer is D. The number of agents in the office is 10 + 5 = 15. The ratio of male agents to the total number of agents is 10:15.

Mathematical Ratio Answer Question #2

The correct answer is D. With *n* being the unknown number, a ratio formula to solve this problem would look like this:

$$\frac{1/4}{2\,\frac{1}{2}} = \frac{12\text{ in}}{n} \qquad n = \frac{12 \times 2\,\frac{1}{2}}{1/4} \qquad n = \frac{12 \times 5/2}{1/4}$$

$$n = \frac{30}{1/4} \qquad n = 30 \div 1/4 \text{ or } 30 \times 4/1$$

$$n = 120'' \text{ or } 10'$$

If you already have a basic understanding of fractions, then a simpler way of solving the problem not using a ratio formula would be:

> 2 = 8/4 and ½ = 2/4
> 2 ½ = 10/4
> 1/4 equals 12 inches and we have ten 1/4
> 10 x 12 = 120 inches or 10 feet

Mathematical Ratio Answer Question #3
The correct answer is C. The ratio 12 to 30 is written 12:30 or 12/30. By dividing both numbers by 2 you can reduce the fraction down to 6/15 or 6:15.

Mathematical Taxation Rate Answer Question #1
The correct answer is D. In order to calculate the tax rate, change the 5% to .05 and multiply that by the dollar amount of $25. $25 x .05 = $1.25 $25.00 + $1.25 = $26.25

Mathematical Taxation Rate Answer Question #2
The correct answer is C. To find the tax rate at which $147,000 would yield $4,410, you must divide the tax amount by the base amount. 4,410 ÷ 147,000 = .03 or 3%.

Mathematical Taxation Rate Answer Question #3
The correct answer is B. To find the dollar amount paid, convert the 2% to .02 then divide the tax paid by the tax rate. $60 ÷ .02 = $3,000.

Cross Multiplying Answer Question #1
The correct answer is C. We know that M/G = Z/x with x being the gallons needed to travel Z miles. Using cross multiplying you have the following formulas:

$$\frac{M}{G} = \frac{Z}{x} \qquad Mx = GZ \qquad x = \frac{GZ}{M}$$

The same thing will work if you had numbers instead of letters. Lets say that M = 400 miles and G = 10 gallons and Z = 200 miles. You can probably figure this out in your head. If a car can travel 400 miles on 10 gallons of gas, it will only need 5 gallons to travel 200 miles. You get the same number using cross multiplying.

$$\frac{400}{10} = \frac{200}{x} \qquad 400\,x = 2000$$

$$x = \frac{2000}{400} \qquad x = 5$$

Chapter III
Federal Law Enforcement Interview

Federal Law Enforcement Interviewing

The interview is usually the first opportunity an agency has to meet you. Therefore, you want to make a good impression. Your goal is to convince them that you possess the qualities of a good police officer. Before you even enter the interview room, there are several things you will want to consider in preparation for the interview.

PREPARING FOR THE INTERVIEW

When applying for a law enforcement position there are usually several forms you have to complete. You will be required to mail some of these forms back to the agency. Other forms may be collected during the interview. Prior to the interview make sure you have accurately completed all of the paperwork. The interviewers will be reviewing the information you have listed. If there are uncompleted portions or you are missing certain forms, this makes you look bad. It may also disqualify you from proceeding any further in the application process. It looks better if you type all of the information. However, neatly printing with a pen is usually acceptable. Remember, the forms you have completed are a reflection of you. It gives the interviewers a little insight into your organizational abilities.

In the days prior to the interview you should review the questions you believe you will be asked as well as your answers to those questions. (These questions and answers will be addressed later in this book.) The Boy Scouts motto of being prepared is very applicable. You do not want to go into the interview winging it. Everyone has a certain degree of nervousness when sitting in front of an interview panel. You want to look your best and sound your best. Avoid becoming tongue-tied by rehearsing your answers.

Make sure you get enough sleep the night before the interview. This will allow you to show up for the interview fully refreshed. If you look tired, you do not look good. Obviously you do not want to sleep in and miss the interview.

On the day of the interview, leave your residence early. Allow yourself enough time to get to the interview. If you should encounter heavy traffic, you will still be able to get there on time. Hopefully, you will arrive early for the interview. This will allow you to collect your thoughts and review your answers. Showing up late for an interview looks bad, and may disqualify you.

LOOKING YOUR BEST

It is a given that most interviewers will expect a man to wear a suit and tie, and a woman to wear a dress or a business suit to the interview. Most of the time, an interviewing panel is prohibited from disqualifying an applicant based on what he or she is wearing. However, if you walk into an interview wearing a pair of blue jeans and a tee shirt, they will find some other reason to write you out. You may look good wearing nice casual slacks, but you will look even better to the panel if you are dressed up. Men, a sport coat is nice, but a matching suit looks better. Women, a skirt is nice, but again a matching skirt and jacket looks better. You want to project a professional image.

As you enter the interviewing room, greet everyone with a firm handshake. Look them in the eyes and smile as you greet them. Remember, you are applying for a law enforcement position. This is a field in which you have to deal with people. You want to show the panel that you are a confident person. Giving someone a weak handshake while looking away is a signal that this occupation is not for you.

You will be asked to sit in a chair. Sit upright using good posture. You may feel more comfortable slouching a little, but the idea is to look good. Place your hands on your lap. Women should cross their legs, but men should refrain from doing so. You do not want to look like you are nervously frozen in the chair. On the other hand, you do not want to look like you are very laid back.

THE INTERVIEW

Your interview will be approximately 30 to 60 minutes in length. You will be questioned by a panel of three to five people. They will probably be seated on one side of a table. On the other side of the table will be your chair. If your chair is in close proximity to the table, you will be sitting at the table with the panel. In most cases, your chair will be approximately six to ten feet away from the table. In this set up, you will not be sitting at the table. The interviewers want you to sit a short distance away from them. This allows them to see your entire body and observe your mannerism. This also prevents you from seeing any notes they may take.

You should answer all of the questions truthfully. If you pass the interview, they will conduct a background investigation. If during their investigation, they discover that you were less than truthful about the smallest of things, you will be disqualified. You are applying for a position in which you have to uphold the law. Therefore, they are looking for integrity.

Most people are a little nervous during a job interview. This is a normal response. To help you relax, pause before answering a question. Take just a brief moment to think about your answer before responding. This will help you to collect your thoughts.

As you answer the questions, speak clearly and loudly. Oral communication is very important in law enforcement. One moment you may be chatting with the public, and the next moment you may be giving forceful verbal commands to a suspect. The panel is assessing your ability to communicate by what you say and how you say it. Speaking in a low tone of voice is not what they want to hear. Meek and mild are not the traits of a good police officer. You only get one chance to make a first impression. So, make a good one.

The panel will be writing throughout the interview. Do not let this bother you. Just because they are writing something down does not mean it is a negative comment. They may be noting your good qualities. They may simply be going through a checklist. You should be more concerned if they do not take any notes.

They should not ask you any questions concerning the law or their specific policies and procedures. You will be taught all of that at their training academy. They will usually begin the interview by verifying the information you provided to them. They will then begin to probe into your past to find out who you are. Lastly, they will ask you some hypothetical questions to judge your reasoning abilities.

Verifying and Probing Questions

VERIFYING QUESTIONS

After reviewing your paperwork, the interview will usually begin with personal data questions. These are usually verifying questions designed to make sure the information they have before them is accurate. They may ask you about your current address and telephone number. They may inquire about your schooling and your current employment. These are questions you should have no problem answering.

PROBING QUESTIONS

After completing the initial verifying phase of the interview, the panel will then begin to ask probing questions. These questions are designed to learn more about you. There are several areas the panel will cover. They may question you about these areas in any order they choose. The following are some standard questions that you may be asked:

What do you know about their agency or department?

If you go into the interview not knowing anything about this particular job, it makes you look bad. The interviewers will ask themselves, "Why would this person apply with us when he or she does not know anything about us?" Lacking this knowledge makes it look like you are applying with any agency just to get your foot into the door. Even if this is true, you do not want to give the appearance that you will use this agency as a stepping stone to a career with another agency. You do not have to know everything about this agency. However, take the time to read up on this agency. Prepare yourself for this question.

Why do you want a career in law enforcement?

If you have always wanted to be a police officer since you were a little kid, then tell them that. Of course, what they really want to know is specifically why do you want to go into law enforcement? If you tell them you want to kick butt and arrest people, you will not pass the interview. If you tell them you like to drive fast cars, you will probably not get hired. Tell them what it is about law enforcement you find attractive. Maybe you like investigative work and would enjoy the challenge of trying to figure out what happened or who did it. Emphasize the high moral standards you have. Protecting your community is something you would like to do.

The panel may also ask why you want a job with their specific agency or department. Do not tell them you always wanted a job with them. Do not tell them they are the best agency even if you feel that way. They will not view your answer as sincere. To them, it looks like you are saying whatever you need to say to get the job. In this case, flattery will get you nowhere. You should tell them what you like about their agency. If you have heard good things about their department, then tell them that. If you know someone who works for them, you can probably mention their name. Tell them that this person had good things to say about them. Be honest but do not try to snowball them. After all, these are police officers that are interviewing you.

Have you applied to any other law enforcement agencies?
The reality is you should apply with every agency you are interested in. Putting all of your eggs in one basket greatly limits your chances of getting into law enforcement. Do not be afraid to answer this question. Tell them every agency you have applied with. They may even ask you what your hiring status is with these other agencies. This does not make you look bad. It shows you are determined to get into law enforcement.

What are your goals?
Usually this refers to your goals in law enforcement. However, they may ask you about your goals in life. The key is to give them some specific goals which are obtainable. Saying that your goal is to be the best police officer or agent that you can be is too vague. Is your goal to be the Director or Chief? This may be your goal and one day you may achieve that status. However, at this point in time, you should start with smaller goals. Tell them your first goal is to get into law enforcement. Your second goal may be to join a specialized field within the department. Perhaps you want to be on the SWAT team or serve as a canine officer or become a supervisor. If you are able to articulate your goals, this makes you a more desirable candidate.

What qualities do you possess?
This question may also be asked in other ways such as, "What are your strong points?" or "What assets will you bring to this agency?" This is your chance to brag about yourself. Everyone has good qualities. Tell them what characteristics you possess that will help you in your job performance. There is a big difference between articulating your strength and boasting. State things as matter-of-fact and avoid embellishing. If you were in a supervisory position, make clear your ability to manage people. Avoid statements such as: "Everyone likes me" or "Everyone knew how well I did this." State your strengths as measurable or documented things. Such statements would be: "There was a low turn over during the time I was a supervisor" or "My boss gave me additional responsibilities." Being liked is an admirable trait but showing your ability to perform is more important. Take some time before the interview and think about your strong points.

What traits do you need to improve upon?
After asking you about your qualities, expect them to ask you about the areas you feel you need to improve. You are not telling them that you are weak or terrible, but you are admitting there are things you could strengthen. This is not the time to air your personal laundry. Choose one or two items, state them and state how you are working to improve them. If you don't mention anything, then you are portraying yourself as being perfect, and the panel will feel that you are not being truthful.

What is your employment history?
The panel will probe into your work history. They will look at the duties you performed in your previous jobs. Share with them any supervisory responsibilities you held. You should mention any accomplishments you had or recognitions you received. Don't fret if your work history consists of minimum wage jobs. You can still show them you are a dependable worker who will get the job done.

If you have worked several jobs, they will ask you why you left one job for another job. Be truthful in your answer. If you left because the new job paid more money or because you did not like what you were doing, then tell them that. If you were fired from a job, they will inquire as to why you were terminated.

If you have just graduated from college and have not yet joined the work force, you probably still have a work history. You should talk about any summer jobs you had, or part-time jobs you had while in school. The panel is looking for reliability. Someone who arrives to work on time and gets the job done. Someone who does not abuse sick leave and has no problems taking orders from a superior.

Tell us about your military service.

If you were in the military, the panel will ask you about your time in the service. They will want to know which branch you served in, what was your highest rank, and what was your duties and responsibilities. If you saw combat, you should mention it to the panel. They will also want to know what type of discharge you received. They may ask you why you left the military.

If you received a medical discharge, the panel will explore this. They will want to know what percentage is your disability. They will also inquire as to the specific nature of your disability. You will need to show that you can perform the full range of duties required of a law enforcement officer.

Are you currently participating in any type of personal fitness program?

Physical fitness is one of the key attributes of a good police officer. The job may require you to chase a suspect, forcefully apprehend a subject or defend yourself from an attacker. These occurrences do not happen every day, but you must be physically prepared for them. The job of a police officer can be very stressful. Stress can lead to several ailments including heart disease. Studies have shown that a body that is in good physical condition is better prepared to handle stress. Therefore, law enforcement agencies are looking for individuals who have developed a healthy and fit lifestyle.

From your general appearance, the panel will be able to assess to a certain degree your physical condition. You will want to provide them with more detailed information on your current level of fitness. You do not have to be a person who works out everyday performing all kinds of cross training exercises. Even if your exercising program has been limited, tell them what you have been doing. It shows them that you care about yourself, and you are doing something to stay in shape. If you have not been exercising, then it would be wise to begin a doctor-approved program. Not only will this help you at the interview, but it will also help you in other stages of the hiring process.

Have you ever been involved in a motor vehicle accident or received a speeding ticket?

You can be sure they will run a computer check to see if you have had any motor vehicle violations. This is one example of where your ability to tell the truth will be verified. Just because you were ticketed for speeding, illegal parking, or for an accident does not mean you are immediately disqualified from obtaining a position with them. Every agency will accept a person who has minor infractions. Nobody is perfect. The agency may have a certain number of violations they will accept. If you exceed the set number, then you are disqualified. For example, four or more speeding tickets in the past two years may be unacceptable. Each agency usually sets the standards they deem appropriate.

What they are looking for is a pattern of deviant behavior. You are applying for a job which enforces the law. If you have demonstrated that you continually break the law, no matter how minor the violation, they are not going to hire you. The other concern is that a police officer spends a great deal of time in a motor vehicle. They want to make sure you can properly handle a vehicle, and that you are not going to get into an accident.

Have you ever been arrested?

As with your driving record, they will run a criminal history through the National Crime Information Center to see if you have a criminal record. Nearly every police agency will not hire you if you have been convicted of a felony charge. A misdemeanor conviction does not necessarily disqualify you for the job. They will inquire as to what type of sentence you received. They will ask you about the details of the case. If this was something you did as a juvenile, then share that with the panel. Their concerns are whether or not this is the only time you were caught. If you were arrested but the charges were later dropped or you were found not guilty, they will question you concerning the charges. Were you truly innocent or did you get off on a technicality? Be prepared for them to inquire about any contacts you had with the police. Maybe you were not arrested but were you detained for questioning?

Do you drink alcohol?
Moderate drinking is acceptable. What they are looking for are those people who drink excessively. Too much drinking can lead to absence from work, poor work performance, bad health, and financial troubles.

Have you ever used an illegal drug?
If you are currently using any illegal drugs, then you will not pass the interview. You cannot break the law while at the same time seek a position which enforces the law. You should openly admit to any previous drug usage. Each agency has certain parameters as to the type of drug and the amount of usage they will accept. If you fall outside of these parameters, there is nothing you can do but apply with another agency.

If you smoked a joint a few times in high school or college, admit to it. This does not necessarily disqualify you. As long as the panel believes this was an infrequent occurrence in your past, and that you are now a responsible adult, you should pass this portion of the interview.

Have you ever sold illegal drugs?
If you have ever dealt in drugs, don't count on getting hired.

Are you currently in any financial debt?
Just because you have an outstanding balance on your credit cards, a car loan, a student loan, and/or mortgage payment does not mean you won't be hired. Most people have borrowed money to pay for the more expensive things in life. What they want to know is if you are credit worthy. A person who is not capable of paying his bills may not be a dependable employee. If you have accumulated a large amount of debt on your credit cards, this too may disqualify you. Accumulating large amounts of unsecured debt shows that you have exercised poor judgement and may be a risk.

Do you have any medical restrictions which would prevent you from performing a full range of duties?
The panel will probably question you about your overall health. They will ask if you are currently taking any medications. They may inquire as to what your vision is. They want to make sure you are physically fit for the job.

Are you willing to take a (drug, medical, psychological, fitness) test?
All they are looking for is a yes answer. If you add anything to your "yes" response or you respond with a "no," then you open yourself up for additional questioning.

Hypothetical Questions

HYPOTHETICAL QUESTIONS

With these type of questions, the panel is trying to determine how you will respond to certain situations. You cannot answer these questions with a simple "yes" or "no." In each question, you will have to perform an action or take a stance. You will have to explain why you would do something or why you would not do something.

The questions are not designed to put you in a "no-win" situation. In each scenario, there are things you should do and things you should not do. You may be faced with the dilemma of wanting to do two things at one time. In this case, you will have to choose the most appropriate course of action.

After the question has been asked, pause for a moment to think about your answer. The point is you shouldn't spout out the first thing that comes to mind. Briefly think about your answer before giving it. They are not testing you on how quickly you respond. They are more concerned with your actions in a given situation. If you take too long thinking, that could be a factor in your rating.

Expect the panel to ask you to justify your actions. They may ask you why you did not do something. This does not mean you gave an incorrect answer. In law enforcement, people are going to get in your face. This is essentially what they are doing by challenging your answer. Do not let this upset you. If you know you gave a good answer, then stick to it.

The questions are usually designed to see how you would perform in areas such as judgement, integrity, supervision, use of force, and dealing with co-workers. The questions may be asked in any order. Usually, there will be several questions for each area of consideration. The following sample questions are typical of what the panel is looking for. Read the sample question twice and then think about how you would answer it. An evaluation of these questions along with appropriate and inappropriate answers are listed at the end of the chapter.

Judgement Scenarios

1. You and your partner are driving a dangerous prisoner to the jail. While en route to the jail, you observe an accident involving three vehicles. It appears that damage to the vehicles is significant. What would you do?

2. While off duty, you go to a convenience store to purchase a few items. No one in the store knows you are a police officer. While you are paying for the items, the cashier engages in a conversation with you. She mentions that she believes she received a counterfeit twenty-dollar bill today. What would you do?

Integrity Scenarios

1. You and your partners are executing a search warrant on a suspected drug dealer's residence. Your team finds illegal drugs and a large amount of money in the house. As your team is securing the contraband in the appropriate evidence bags, you observe one team member place some of the money into his pocket. What would you do?

2. You are investigating the illegal coping and selling of videotaped movies. While interviewing the owner of one of the suspected video stores, he offers you several free rentals. What would you do?

Supervision Scenarios

1. Everyone in your office has had the chance to participate on a "special detail." When another detail comes up, your supervisor gives it to a co-worker who has already been on a similar assignment. This pattern continues two more times with you getting passed over for any "special details." What would you do?

2. After working in one office for five years, you receive a new supervisor. After six months under her supervision, it appears that she does not like you. You discuss this with her, but she acts like nothing will change. At the end of the year, she gives you a low rating. You talk to her about your rating, but she appears to be inattentive. What would you do?

Use-of-Force Scenarios

1. You are by yourself driving through an area that has several retail stores. You witness a man grab a woman's purse. The two of them are struggling for control of the purse. The man starts to strike the woman with his hands. What would you do?

2. You and several other officers are attempting to arrest a subject at his residence. As you are walking up to the house, the front door opens and the subject appears. He steps out of the doorway and onto the front porch. He has a gun in his hand and he begins shooting at you. What would you do?

Dealing with Co-Workers Scenarios

1. For the past several months, there have been many assignments which required someone to work late at night. Everyone in your office has done their share of working late hours except for one person. His continual refusal to work after hours is causing a strain with his co-workers. What would you do?

2. There are two co-workers in your office who do not like each other. Their refusal to work together is causing problems in scheduling assignments. Morale in the office is low because of their bickering. What would you do?

Answers to the Hypothetical Questions

Judgement Answers

1. The dilemma with this question is, should you stop to help those involved in the accident, or should you continue to do your job transporting this prisoner? If you state that you would stop to provide assistance, the panel will question you about leaving your partner alone with the prisoner. They may also point out that this could be a setup in order to free the prisoner. If you state that you would not stop to help those involved in the accident, the panel may ask you, "You mean you would let these people die?"

   Be sure to convey to the panel that you recognize the situation you are in. You would like to help those in need, but you also have a duty to maintain control of this prisoner. If they have not mentioned it, you should tell them that this accident may be a ruse designed to ambush you and your partner.

   Since the prisoner is dangerous, you should probably continue on to the jail. However, you will provide assistance to the accident victims by radioing for medical emergency services. Remember, there are other ways to help besides physically lending a hand.

2. There is nothing wrong with asking to look at the suspected counterfeit bill. Unless you are a Secret Service agent, you should not take possession of the bill. There is no sense in getting involved in the chain of custody. If the bill appears to be phony, tell the cashier to report it to the Secret Service. You may also want to notify them.

   The key to this question is to notify the proper authorities. Even though you are a police officer, it may not be your responsibility or jurisdiction to investigate this type of crime.

Integrity Answers

1. A bad answer would be, "I would report it to my supervisor." The first thing you should do is confront your co-worker. Tell him what you observed, and ask him what he did with the money. Suggest to the panel that perhaps he logged it into another evidence bag.

   The panel will probably ask you, "What would you do if he says he did not put any money into his pocket?" You should tell them that if your co-worker continued to deny taking the money, you would then notify your supervisor.

2. Tell the panel that you recognize this could be a bribe. Even if the owner was not bribing you, it would be inappropriate to accept such an offer. Therefore, you will not accept the free video rentals. You should make a note of what transpired in case this would be used against the store owner at a later time.

Supervision Answers

1. Chain of command is important in law enforcement. Therefore, you should not state that you would immediately notify your supervisor's boss. You should go to your supervisor and ask why you have not received a special detail. Maybe he overlooked you, or maybe there is something you need to do.

   If the problem persists or you have not received a satisfactory explanation from your supervisor, you should then go to the next supervisory level.

2. This is similar to the previous question in that you should try to work things out with your supervisor before going to the next boss. This question differs in that your supervisor is a woman. Some people, men and women, have a problem taking orders from a woman. The panel is looking to see if you react to the fact that your boss is a woman. You should not make any reference about her sex.

Use-of-Force Answers

1. There is nothing wrong with getting on the radio and calling for assistance. However, in this scenario you should do more than that. Get out of your car and identify yourself as a police officer. Order the man to let go of the woman. If the man does not stop attacking the woman, you are going to have to physically stop him. You would then place him under arrest.

   The panel may ask you if you would draw your weapon. In this type of situation, you probably cannot shoot the attacker. If you see no weapons in his hands, then your gun will probably remain holstered. You may not know what type of intermediate weapons this agency allows it's personnel to carry. However, you can still suggest that you may use a baton or pepper spray on the subject if he refuses to stop the attack.

2. The first thing you should do is seek cover. The subject is firing his weapon at you, so there is no time to give verbal commands for him to stop. You should draw your gun and return fire. You are attempting to stop the subject's aggression. When it is safe to do so, you should get on the radio and call for assistance.

Dealing with Co-workers Answers

1. You should confront the co-worker. It would probably be better if you did this as a group and not individually. Share with him the burden he is placing on everyone by his refusal to work some of the late hours. If he would work a few of the late night hours, it would be helpful to others in the office. Tell the panel that you hope things could be worked out. If the panel suggests that things are not working out, then you will have to talk with your supervisor.

2. Again the key is to talk to both co-workers. Try to find out what the problem is. Arrange for the two of them to have a meeting with each other in order to resolve their differences. Suggest that they do not have to love each other, but they need to work with each other. The panel is looking to see if

you would make an effort to help in these situations. Going straight to your boss is not always the best answer.

ESSAY QUESTION

Many interviews will include an evaluation of your writing skills. The panel will solicit from you a writing sample in one of two ways. You may be asked to answer, in writing, a general broad question. Instead of a question, you may be given a picture and asked to describe in writing, what you see in the picture. This is usually done before the oral interview, and you have approximately 30 minutes to complete the exercise.

The panel will probably not question you about your writing sample unless there is something they do not understand. The panel will grade your writing ability. This score will be part of your overall interview rating. Neatness should not be a factor. However, you want to submit something that they can read. If your handwriting is terrible, then consider printing your essay. You can write as much as you want. One or two pages, consisting of approximately four paragraphs, is acceptable.

Your writing sample will be graded on grammar, spelling, punctuation, sentence structure, organization and clarity of thought. They do not expect you to be a professional writer. They are grading your ability to effectively communicate in writing. Report writing is something police officers have to do on a regular basis.

DO YOU HAVE ANY QUESTIONS?

The interview will usually end with the panel asking you if you have any questions. They will probably not answer questions like, "Did I pass?" or "How well did I do?" They will state that they have to forward your information to another person who will make the final decision.

You should ask them when and how you will be notified as to the results of your interview. You may want to ask them what is the next step in the hiring process. Ask how many people they plan to hire this year and when is the next recruit training class.

Keep in mind that the interview is not over yet. After you leave, the panel may discuss their overall impression of you. Therefore, you want to leave on a positive note. Ask a few questions to show you are interested in obtaining a job with them. Thank them for the opportunity to interview, and shake their hands as you leave.

DID YOU PASS OR FAIL THE INTERVIEW?

There is no sure way to know immediately if you passed the interview. Most of the time, the interviewing panel knows if you passed or failed. As previously stated, they usually will not reveal this to you. If you failed, you will receive notification in the mail within the next few weeks stating that you did not meet their interviewing standards.

If you passed the interview, there will be additional steps that you will have to complete before they offer you a job. The next phase may be to get a medical examination or complete a physical fitness test. Some agencies will not send you a letter stating that you have passed the interview. Instead, you will receive notification that you are scheduled to take one of these additional tests. If they continue to consider you for a position, then you know you passed the interview. A background investigation will be conducted after you have passed the interview. If your friends tell you that the police have been asking about you, this too will let you know you passed the interview.

Each year, thousands of people apply for federal law enforcement jobs. Those who meet the minimum qualifications and can pass the written entrance examination will probably receive an interview. Approximately 50% of those applicants will not pass the interview. By properly preparing yourself, and using the guidelines and tips outlined in this book, you will increase your chances of successfully completing a law enforcement interview.

Chapter IV
Other Factors in the Selection Process

OTHER FACTORS IN THE SELECTION PROCESS

Passing the written entrance test and the interview are two of the biggest steps toward achieving a federal law enforcement job. However, there are still several other phases of the selection process you will have to complete. Some of these phases you can prepare for, others may have already been determined for you by your past actions.

PSYCHOLOGICAL TEST

Some agencies will give a psychological test to determine if you have the personality traits suitable for police work. There are several forms of testing. Each agency can use whatever type of test they deem appropriate. One of the most common tests consists of approximately 400 statements that you will have to agree or disagree with. Some of the statements may seem ridiculous while others will clearly focus on your character. What they are looking for is consistency in your viewpoints with regard to your honesty, loyalty, and dependability. Therefore, you should answer all of the questions truthfully. Do not try to outsmart the test by giving answers you think they want to see.

MEDICAL EXAMINATION

All agencies will give their candidates a medical examination to determine their fitness for duty. The medical examination is usually conducted by a physician hired by the agency although some agencies may allow you to go to your own doctor. They will usually pay for all of the costs associated with the physical exam. The exam is a basic physical checkup. The doctor will review your medical history to see if you have had any previous problems or past surgeries. For example, if you had reconstructive surgery to fix a broken jaw, you may not pass the physical. Most training programs include defensive tactics classes which may require you to spar with a partner. One shot to the chin and you may need surgery again. The exam will also determine if you have any current ailments which may preclude you from employment. Your vision will be checked to make certain you meet the agency's minimum standards. The doctor will also state if you are cleared to take the physical fitness test.

PHYSICAL FITNESS TEST

Most agencies will give a candidate a physical fitness or physical agility test. This is usually done sometime after being cleared by the medical examination. A lot of the agencies have developed their physical fitness test based on the research conducted by the Coopers Aerobic Institute in Dallas, Texas. The test will usually consist of performing push-ups and sit-ups for one minute each, a 1.5 mile run, a sit-and-reach flexibility test, and a skin-fold pinch test to measure your body fat. The minimum passing score is usually based on your age and gender. However, some agencies have a minimum standard that applies to all persons regardless of their age and sex.

In some cases, you may be given only one week notice before taking the fitness test. Therefore, if you are not in the best of shape, it is a good idea to begin an exercise program as soon as you start applying for a job. If you fail part of the test, some agencies may allow you to retest at a later date. Others will only give you one chance at passing it.

POLYGRAPH TEST

Many agencies require that an applicant take a polygraph test, also referred to as a lie detector test. The polygraph is able to determine if you are being truthful by monitoring four areas of your body: your heart rate, blood pressure, breathing rate, and perspiration. For most people, knowingly telling a lie creates a degree of stress in their body. For some people, this stress will surface causing them to blush. Other people may be able to do a better job at concealing their deception. However, even the slightest physiological change can be detected by the polygraph.

Before giving the polygraph test, the administrator will conduct a pretest interview. During this time he will explain the testing procedures and how the polygraph equipment works. He will also review the questions to be asked during the polygraph examination. The pretest interview may last from 30 to 90 minutes.

To begin the test, the examiner will attach several components to your body. A monitoring device will be placed around your chest and abdomen to record your breathing rate. A cuff will be placed on your upper arm to record your heart rate and blood pressure. Metal electrodes will be placed on your ring and index finger to monitor your perspiration. There is nothing painful about the test.

The questions will be short and require you to give a "yes" or "no" answer. You will not be able to explain your answers because the questions do not require an explanation, and the polygraph requires you to give "yes" and "no" answers. Once the test begins, the examiner will ask you several control questions. These are questions that everyone should be able to answer truthfully. Questions about your name, age and the city you live in are designed to show the examiner what a truthful response from you looks like as recorded by the polygraph. You will also be asked a question that is designed to stir your emotions. One possible question may be "Have you ever stolen anything valued less than $20.00?" Most people will have to honestly answer this question with a "yes." The examiner wants you to be slightly embarrassed because he wants a truthful answer that has some emotions attached to it. Some examiners will ask you to purposefully answer a question with a lie. They want to see how the polygraph records your deceptive response.

During the test the examiner may ask the same question several times. This does not mean that he does not believe your answer. He is creating several charts that he can use to make his opinion. Typical questions that will be used to determine your truthfulness will have to do with your drug usage, drug sales, theft of property or money, and contact with foreign officials. The total testing time including the pretest interview may last from 2 to 3 hours.

The best thing you can do to pass the polygraph test is to answer the questions truthfully, and try and remain calm throughout the test. If you have a clean background, then you do not have anything to worry about. The examiner knows that most people will be a little apprehensive. He will consider this in his analysis of your scores.

BACKGROUND INVESTIGATION

All agencies will conduct a background investigation on each candidate they are considering hiring. Investigators will look into your character examining a variety of things including your honesty, integrity, financial status, drug and alcohol usage, and loyalty to the United States. This will be done by interviewing individuals who know you and by reviewing various records.

One of the first groups of people they will interview is the references you have listed on your application. Everyone is going to list their friends and family who they trust will say good things about them. Therefore, after interviewing your friends, the investigators will ask them for the names of other individuals who know you. Hopefully they will have good things to say about you too.

The investigators will also interview your former employers and co-workers to establish your work habits. They will look at your job performance to see if it is satisfactory. They will examine the number of times you called in sick to see if you are a dependable worker, and to see if you abuse your sick leave.

They will also interview your neighbors and perhaps your school mates to determine your reputation. It is not unusual for investigators to speak with people who had contact with you ten years ago. Even though these individuals may not know what you are currently doing, the investigators are looking at your past to establish a pattern of behavior. They are also verifying how truthful you were during the interview and in the paperwork that you have completed.

The other phase of the background investigation will be a record's check. The investigators will look to see if you have a criminal history, or if your contact with law enforcement officials coincides with what you stated in the interview. They will review financial records to see if you have good credit or if you are extremely in debt. They may look at auto insurance records to see if you are a responsible driver.

What can you do to pass the background investigation? First make sure you complete all of the required forms accurately. You need to provide the investigators with the correct contact information for your references and former employers. These are the people you want them to interview. Secondly make sure your financial matters are in order. There is nothing wrong with having a mortgage, car or student loan payment. The problem arises when you miss a payment. Be certain that you are current with your financial obligations. Too much debt may be a reflection of your poor judgement.

Chapter V
The Training Academy

THE TRAINING ACADEMY

Except for the Federal Bureau of Investigation and the Drug Enforcement Administration, all federal law enforcement agencies conduct part, if not all, of their training at the Federal Law Enforcement Training Center (FLETC) located in Brunswick, Georgia. Basic training usually consists of a nine-week Criminal Investigator course, or an eight-week Police Training course. Classes are taught by former agents/officers who are now full-time FLETC instructors, and by current agents who are detailed from their agency to the FLETC. Once a recruit completes the basic FLETC training, he or she will then receive specific agency training. The agency training may be conducted at another facility. It will generally last from five to ten weeks and is taught by agents from your agency. Throughout both phases of training, students are generally tested in five areas of instruction: written examinations, firearms qualifications, driving qualifications, physical fitness, and practical exercises.

The written examinations are designed to test your ability to grasp the classroom instruction. Usually there will be three to four multiple choice tests during the training. You will receive a variety of classes such as constitutional law, search and seizure, use of force, interviewing techniques, report writing, surveillance, operational planning, improvised exploding devices, policy & procedures, and radio communications. With most questions, you can usually quickly eliminate two answers as incorrect. However, to make certain you know the material, two of the answers may sound very similar. Therefore, it is important to take good notes in the classroom and to study for each test. 70% is usually the lowest passing score. If you fail a test, you may be entitled to a remedial test which you must pass. Most agencies only allow for one remedial test throughout the entire training program. In each Criminal Course, there are usually several people who will fail because of poor academics. While the Training Academy may have a college atmosphere, you must remember that you are no longer in college. You will not be taking any classes that seem insignificant and have no bearing on your life. This is your life! You are studying to be a federal agent. If you can pass the Training

Academy, you are on your way to a high paying job with good benefits. Therefore, the choice is yours. While in training you can party all night, or you can get serious about the career that lies a head of you.

Statistics show that most police officers never discharge their firearm in the line of duty. However, if an officer needs to use his firearm, it can be a matter of life and death for the officer, for the suspect and for the general public. Therefore, all agencies will provide their recruits with a significant number of hours of firearms training. Students will have to qualify with a variety of weapons including a handgun, shotgun, rifle and perhaps a submachine gun. It is common to have recruits who have never shot a gun or have only occasionally fired a weapon. Firearms instructors actually like this because they can mold the person into becoming a good shooter. They will teach you the proper way to stand, hold the gun, align your sites and use good trigger control. Experienced shooters who have no formal firearms training have sometimes developed bad habits which are hard to change.

For most agencies, qualifying with a firearm involves shooting at a stationary paper target. When the target turns and faces you, you will then draw your weapon and fire a prescribed number of rounds. When the target faces away, you then holster your weapon. You will probably not be shooting at moving targets for qualification. A typical course of fire consists of 300 rounds with 70% or a score of 210 as qualifying. Most students are able to satisfactorily complete this phase of training.

All agencies require that their agents have a valid driver's license. You will spend a lot of time in the car conducting a surveillance, driving to an interview or perhaps transporting a prisoner. Some agencies may have you take a basic driver's test to make certain you possess fundamental driving skills. The main area of concern is operating your vehicle at a high rate of speed. Most agencies will have their recruits participate in a high speed pursuit driving course. This involves classroom instruction on how to handle a car when driving fast. It is then followed by driving a car around a track at various speeds. In the testing phase, the students must complete several laps around the track in a certain time period.

There are usually plenty of opportunities to practice and time yourself.

Students may also be taught the proper ways to execute a bootleg or J-turn with a vehicle. This involves driving a car either forward or backwards, and then suddenly turning the vehicle 180 degrees. This allows you to quickly turn your car around and retreat in case of an attack. You will be taught the proper ways to use your brakes and emergency brakes and how to steer the car into such a turn. Successfully demonstrating the technique is usually required. Only on a rare occasion does someone fail the driving portion of training.

Physical fitness plays a very important part in a police officer's career. The job sometimes requires working long hours. An agent who is in good physical condition will remain more alert as he or she is working ten to twelve hour shifts. Sitting in a car, at a desk or at a post for long periods of time can lead to lower back problems. This is why most agencies have a sit and reach test to determine the flexibility in your lower back. The more limber you are the less chance of lower back injuries. There is also the chance you may have to pursue a suspect. Therefore, cardiovascular endurance is very important. Once you catch the suspect you need to have the strength to control and apprehend him. As mentioned in chapter four, the physical fitness test usually consists of push-ups and sit-ups performed in one minute, a 1.5 mile, sit and reach flexibility test and a skin fold pinch test to determine your fat. Agencies may also have other areas of testing such as climbing over a wall, climbing a rope or an agility speed test. Passing scores are usually based on your age and gender.

Besides the physical fitness test, there will be several physical fitness classes that you will have to complete. There may be early morning or late afternoon runs and calisthenic sessions. You will also receive plenty of instruction in defensive tactics. The best thing you can do to prepare for the physical training is to get in shape before going to the training academy. Many candidates make the mistake of believing that they will get in shape while at the academy. On the first day of physical training your class may go for a five mile run. If you are not able to run for five miles, then you will fall behind only to be verbally motivated by the instructors. You may be able to handle the instructor's words of encouragement, but you may not be able to deal with the injuries that arise from being out of shape. The most common injury in a physical fitness training program is shin splints. This pain in the shin area is usually caused by a sudden increase in running. To get shin splints while in training will make your training more difficult. There are thousands of people who want the job you have been offered. Therefore, you are not in a position to tell the instructors at the training academy that you do not feel like running today. Most people who fail the physical fitness portion of training do so because of injuries.

The final area of evaluation will be a variety of practical exercises that you will have to successfully complete. This may include handcuffing and searching techniques, administering first aid and CPR, interviewing individuals, building searches, conducting a surveillance, report writing, warrant execution and use of force. Most of these are graded on a pass / fail basis. If the instructor feels that you did not satisfactorily complete the exercise, then you will be given an opportunity to participate in the exercise again. Because of the amount of time in which you have to prepare, most students are able to easily pass the practical exercises.

Helpful Hints to Obtaining a Federal Law Enforcement Job

When applying for a federal law enforcement job, take as many tests or fill out as many applications as possible. Do not limit yourself to one agency. Apply with whomever is hiring. You can always turn them down if you later decide that this isn't the job for you.

Even if OPM administers the written test, write or call the agencies you are interested in. They may be able to give you an idea of when they will be hiring and the dates of the next written test. Even if the test is closed, if the agency really likes you they may petition OPM for authorization to give you the written entrance examination.

After you have taken an entrance test, make an occasional telephone call to see what your status is in the hiring process. Let them know you are interested.

When written entrance examinations are opened, sometimes more than 5000 people will apply for several hundred positions. Don't let the large number of applicants discourage you. Consider the following:

- A lot of people do not pass the written test.
- Many people who take the written exam are not qualified for the job. Later on during the hiring process they are notified that they do not meet the educational/experience requirements.
- Nearly half of the applicants do not pass the interview.
- Some people do not pass the medical examination.
- Some people do not pass the polygraph test.
- Some people do not pass the psychological exam.
- Some people do not pass the physical fitness test.
- Some people do not pass the background investigation.

- If you score an average rating on the test, a lot of people will have scored lower than you. You will move onto the next phase of the hiring of the process before they will.
- Some test scores are only good for one year unless you renew your score at the end of the year. Many people forget to renew their scores and are taken off the eligibility list.

When you add all of these up, your chances of getting hired begin to look better.

Also Published By PoliceEmployment.com

State Handgun Laws
State Trooper Career Employment Guide
State Correctional Officer Career Employment Guide
Ground Fighting Techniques For Law Enforcement Officers (video and manual)

For more information on these publications, visit our web site at:
www.PoliceEmployment.com

or you can request a flyer by writing to us
PoliceEmployment.com
P.O. Box 2090
Winterville, NC 28590-2090